then & now

BACKTRACKING AROUND
MILLBAY, SALTASH & THE TAMAR

written & compiled by

Bernard Mills

British Library Cataloguing in Publication Data
Mills, Bernard –
Backtracking Around: Millbay, Saltash and the Tamar
1. England - Devon - Plymouth - History
2. Railroads - England - Plymouth Region - History - 20th century ;
3. Railroads - England - Plymouth Region - History - 20th century - Pictorial works ;
Dewey: 385.0942358

I. Title
647.9'5'0942358
ISBN 978-0-9934812-3-9

Designed by Ben Robinson

First published November 2016

OTHER SIMILAR TITLES FROM PEN & INK:

Plymouth Then & Now - 2004
Then & Now: The Changing Face of Plymouth - 2006
Then & Now: Plymouth - An Ever Evolving City - 2009
Backtracking Around: Friary, Laira and the Plym - 2013

Published by
Pen & Ink Publishing
34 New Street
Barbican
Plymouth PL1 2NA
01752 228120

www.chrisrobinson.co.uk

Printed & bound in Great Britain by
Latimer Trend & Company Ltd
Estover Close
Plymouth PL6 7PL
Devon

Introduction

Southern green meets GWR chocolate and cream. A train from the former Southern Line passes a former (and by now redundant) GWR Signal Box, a picture which carries the essence of the story of the two rival lines making their way through the west side of Plymouth to the River Tamar. Ivatt tank 41 310 is seen at North Road West with the 1322 Saturdays-only Tavistock north Plymouth. *AC/BM Collection, 30 May 1961*

Welcome to Back Tracking Around Millbay, Saltash and the Tamar, the second book looking at the railways in and around the City of Plymouth. As with the previous volume, it is set in the era in which I know the system – from the late 1950s to the present day.

An alternative title for the series could be The Changing Face of Plymouth, for the changes off the rails are many and in some cases even more apparent than those on them.

We again start our journey at Plymouth Station, the former North Road built, rather grudgingly, by the GWR in 1877 to accommodate the LSWR which had entered the scene in 1876 by way of the GWR Tavistock and Launceston Branch. Our route this time takes us to the west of the station, covering the complexities of the Cornwall Loop Triangle and into Millbay and the Docks. Returning to Cornwall Loop Junction, we follow the former still extant and greatly changed former GWR main line through the western suburbs to the River Tamar, Brunel's masterpiece and a detailed look at the anatomy of a wayside station, Saltash where I learnt my trade as a booking and railway clerk. We then go out on the Tamar Road Bridge to look down on the former LSWR route and follow that back through St Budeaux, and the now completely expunged route through Weston Mill and Ford to Devonport Junction.

The railways on the western side of the City are not as complex as those on the eastern side where the two systems competed for access to the Quays and the River Plym. Running west from the present Plymouth Station, once they had gone their separate ways at Devonport Junction, the two main lines interweaved their way out to the Tamar with the SR route passing under the GWR route no less than three times.

Branch lines were few on this side of the City, due no doubt to the greater part of the eastern bank of the River Tamar being occupied by Devonport Dockyard and the Naval Base. The GWR had its line to Millbay and the Docks, the SR served Stonehouse Pool. The Dockyard was served by the still extant (but infrequently used these days) branch which still joins the main line to the north of Keyham. This connects with the Dockyard's own once extensive, passenger carrying and somewhat secretive internal system hidden mostly from the public eye, restricted in access and photography for security reasons, but as we shall see such defences were breached on occasions by the railway enthusiast fraternity!

The only other branch was the very short one at St Budeaux to Bull Point, another rarely photographed line as Bull Point was an armaments depot. Camera touting railway photographers were as welcome anywhere within sniffing distance to that as is now a motorist in a Plymouth bus lane.

Thereafter, as one line crossed the Tamar and the other hugged its banks, the two railways went their separate ways. One headed west, and still does, to serve the Royal Duchy, the other east now only to reach the Upper Tamar Valley but, until May 1968, this was a main line which skirted Northern Dartmoor on its inland route to Exeter. How valuable would that be today, and who knows with all the problems at Dawlish the inland route to Plymouth could one day be rebuilt. We wait and see.

This book, like its companion for the eastern side, does not set out to be a history of the railways of Plymouth, a complex story already told elsewhere. Briefly the route from Laira Green to the terminus at Millbay opened on 4 April 1849. A decade later saw the Cornwall Railway open its main line from Cornwall Junction to Truro on 4 May 1859: through trains from east to west and vice versa were, of course, obliged to reverse in Millbay. Six weeks later to the east of the City came the opening of the South Devon and Tavistock Railway on 22 June 1859, extended to Launceston on 1 July 1865.

It should be noted that all these routes had been built to Brunel's seven feet and a quarter inch broad gauge, but in 1876 an interloper arrived on the scene in the form of the London and South Western Railway, a great rival of the GWR and its associated Companies and built to the standard gauge of four feet eight and a half inches. Having arrived at Lydford on 12 October 1874, the LSWR gained access to Plymouth by running powers over the broad gauge branch from Lydford, enforcing the installation of mixed gauge, a cumbersome arrangement, then by passing Millbay by means of the Cornwall Loop and its viaduct to run a short distance over the Cornwall Railway to Devonport Junction. Here the LSWR reached their handsome terminus at Devonport by a short branch opening on 18 May 1876.

Mostly to accommodate the LSWR in its desire to serve Plymouth as well as Devonport, it was agreed that a new joint station would be built at North Road. Planned as a stone structure, it was built of wood because of the GWR delay in starting it and the LSWR impatience for its opening. At first the GWR considered the new station, opened on 28 March 1877, an impediment, but soon came to realise its importance particularly in obviating the need for Cornwall-bound trains to avoid the reversal at Millbay, although it would not be until 1929 that the overnight Penzance-Paddington train would become the last to undertake this routine.

North Road Station was enlarged in 1908, rebuilding started in 1938 and was interrupted by the World War II, resuming in 1956 and was eventually opened by Dr Beeching in March 1963 Due to bomb damage to the adjoining goods station and thus the need to use the platforms for freight, Millbay was closed to passengers on 23 April 1941. With the closure of Friary to passengers on 15 September 1958 the 'North Road' suffix was dropped, although to may locals the station is still known as 'North Road'.

It was the Plymouth, Devonport & South Western Junction Railway, a company with ambitions which at times worried the authorities at Waterloo, that built the next line into Plymouth. The independent route from Lydford entered the City by coming down the east bank of the River Tamar from the Bere Peninsula to pass under Brunel's Saltash Bridge and make its own (and it must be said, heavily engineered) way to Devonport where the former terminus became a through station, opening on 2 June 1890, with trains going to Friary from 1 July 1891. Both the PDSWJ and the LSWR were absorbed by the Southern Railway in the Grouping of 1923. The line from St Budeaux to Devonport was closed completely as from 7 September 1964 trains diverting to the original Cornwall Railway route by means of the upgraded World War II connection here between the two systems. Devonport Kings Road reverted to its former role as the terminus of the short branch from Devonport Junction albeit for freight only until total closure on 7 March 1971. Four months later the line from North Road to Millbay Docks closed on 30 June 1971.

In the present day, west of Plymouth station, all that survives is the main line out to Saltash with the connection to the Naval Base at Keyham and, what has been, since May 1968, the Gunnislake Branch. Reminders of the Millbay system and the SR route from St Budeaux to Devonport are few, indeed I know of local people who do not realise the railway once ran through Weston Mill. Other dates are mentioned where relevant in the appropriate text.

The rivalry between the Southern and Great Western systems will be widely evident throughout this book, but there were some curiosities. Each of the two stations at St Budeaux had a booking office on each platform. When in 1952 both were placed under the control of the same Station Master, the latter had the unique distinction of overseeing four platforms and four booking offices!

The majority of the illustrations are my own work, or from a collection where I hold the copyright, and some are from the joint collection I have with my good friend Amyas Crump, these identified as AC/BM Collection. Where pictures are not from my own resources, these are individually acknowledged in the captions. My thanks are due to many people for their help and assistance, Chris and Clare Robinson and their team for his faith in me to produce and publish the finished article, Roger Geach for help with picture scanning and his train identification skills along with Martin Street. Jeremy Clark as ever for his editorial input and proof reading, Paul Burkhalter for sharing his detailed knowledge of the Dockyard system and arranging for a visit to update the pictures, Bruce Hunt from Saltash Heritage for sharing his vast knowledge of the Cornish town and its ferry, also Plymouth bomb damage in the Second War. Terry Nicholls for help with Millbay information and provision of rare pictures of the railway through Weston Mill, Sid Sponheimer for a couple of rare views of the SR main line and Brian Moseley with what is best described as heroic research with information on World War II bombing.

I must also mention the assistance of my good friend Mike Hunt over the years together with Dave Mitchell, Colin Marsden, Steve and Ron Andrews, Barry Lucas and John Fissler for help with signalling matters, and my friends in the Cornwall Railway Society in particular Keith Jenkin. Two people I dearly wish I could express thanks to in person are the late Larry Crosier and Ivor Hocking. I am the custodian of Ivor's pictures and some appear in this volume. If have left anyone out I apologise for so many people have contributed in so many ways to ensure accuracy. Then there are my railway colleagues over the last 50 years and more to thank for their knowledge, help and friendship and it is their, as well as my, memories I have tried to record for posterity.

Many of the images used in this volume and many more from my collection can be purchased as digital copies and prints from; www.classictractionimages.weebly.com

(Opposite page) The author visiting the Royal Albert Bridge signal box, June 1973

The view from Millbay signal box looking south, July 1966

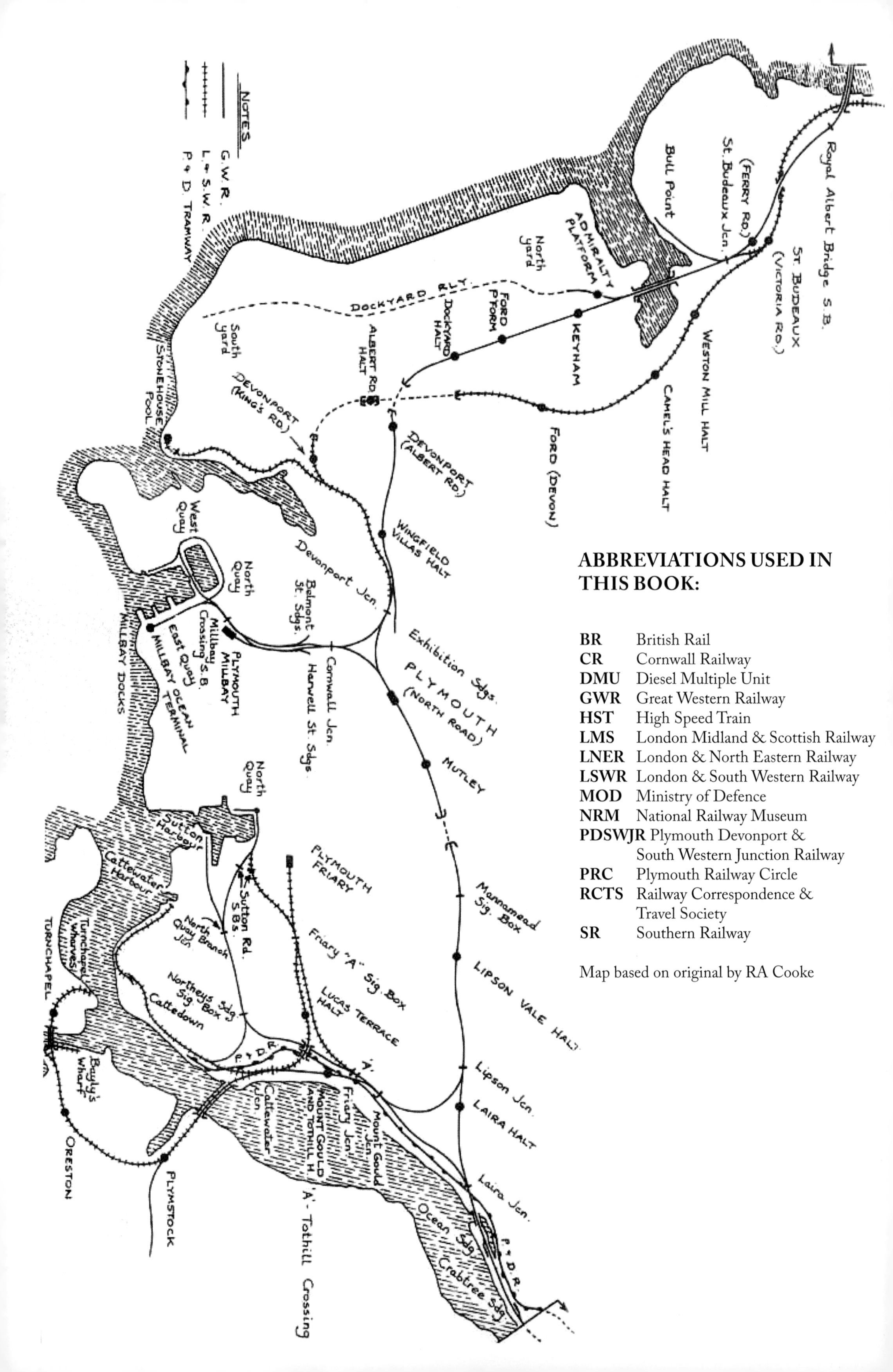

ABBREVIATIONS USED IN THIS BOOK:

BR British Rail
CR Cornwall Railway
DMU Diesel Multiple Unit
GWR Great Western Railway
HST High Speed Train
LMS London Midland & Scottish Railway
LNER London & North Eastern Railway
LSWR London & South Western Railway
MOD Ministry of Defence
NRM National Railway Museum
PDSWJR Plymouth Devonport & South Western Junction Railway
PRC Plymouth Railway Circle
RCTS Railway Correspondence & Travel Society
SR Southern Railway

Map based on original by RA Cooke

BACKTRACKING AROUND
MILLBAY, SALTASH & THE TAMAR

An historic moment at Plymouth Station as the founder member of the Plymouth Railway Circle, the late Harold Liddle, places the headboard (which he had made) to the front of 'West Country' 34002 Salisbury, prior to the departure of the last BR steam-hauled train to Penzance, the PRC/RCTS 'Cornubian' Rail Tour which GWR 2-8-0 2887 had worked down from Exeter. This would also be the first occasion a Bulleid Pacific would go west of Truro. In the crowd to the left are the young author (identified by his red pullover), my late father is next to me, and in the group behind I can see Derrick Organ. Under the station canopy wearing his bowler hat, the Station Master, Ted Savoury, keeps an eye on the proceedings. By this time he had already confirmed my employment to join British Rail at the Station and he reminded me I was to report for duty on Monday 27 July!

An interesting anecdote: the then Naval Chaplain at HMS *Drake* was the Revd Sinclair, a fiery Irish man of the cloth and was also a member of the PRC. With minutes to spare before the train went on its way, I do recall seeing a chauffeur-driven official Naval car pull up outside the station, the Revd Sinclair then dashing to platform 3 with a beaming smile exclaiming, "*that is the shortest sermon they will ever get!*" *3 May 1964*

Contents

Contents

As in the previous volume Backtracking Around Friary, Laira and the Plym, we start our journey at Plymouth Station, but now we are looking in the other direction, to the west. It's a rather untidy scene as a Plymouth-Saltash auto (push/pull with the driver able to control the engine from the cab of the coaches) train stands at Platform 5 with coach W166W nearest the camera. The normal mode of operation was to pull two coaches out to Saltash, or various other destinations as far as Doublebois at certain times of the day, and push back. For peak periods additional auto trailers would be added to the front of the train. Such trains, with the engine in the middle, were known as 'sandwich trains'. Often for the mid-morning and lunch-time peaks, a single trailer was retained on the Saltash end. For rush hours there would be two trailers either side of the 6400 Class pannier tank, and these trains carried up to 500 passengers. To many these trains were known as 'The Saltash Motor', (and to the local train spotters somewhat unkindly as 'The Saltash Stinker'). Beyond the leading auto coach the former North Road West Signal Box can be spotted alongside with a fine signal gantry. These were overtaken by the still extant Plymouth Panel Signal Box in November 1960. *June 1959*

A much tidier and instantly recognisable scene 50 years later, and someone has picked up all the litter!
The trains may not be so interesting these days, but they are very colourful. Voyager 220 013 awaits departure to the east with the 1425 to Edinburgh and, such is the transformation of long distance travel, one can have lunch in Plymouth and with a bit of luck catch 'last orders' in an Edinburgh bar. The Voyagers also have nicknames, but these are not ones I would not dare to put into print. Although taken seven years ago, there has been no change in the present day view. *30 July 2009*

LOOKING WEST FROM THE STATION TOWER BLOCK

We are looking down from the ninth floor of the Station Tower Block to the west, with the still-extant Panel Signal Box to the immediate bottom left. Directly opposite on the right, Royal Mail vehicles are parked in the carpark of the former sorting office. Stonehouse Creek once flowed up to here, under both viaducts, and barges were tied up at a wharf at this point as late as the 1890s. Railway-wise we have a grandstand view of the Cornwall Loop Triangle, and small 'Prairie' tank 4555 engaged on station pilot duties adding a bit of steam to the atmosphere. The route of 1849 to Millbay diverges to the left. To the right is the Cornwall Loop and its viaduct of the same name, opened in 1876. The triangle is completed by the Cornwall Railway route of 1859 from Cornwall Junction over Stonehouse Pool Viaduct to Cornwall Loop Junction. Stonehouse Pool Viaduct is so named, of course, because when first built it did cross the waters of the creek, whose course from the sea is easily traceable by the reclaimed Victoria Park clearly evident leading back to Millbridge. Note, just adjacent to the Millbay lines, the locomotive Servicing Point. These are all locations we shall be inspecting on our journey. *AC/BM Collection, May 1963*

Only three years separate these two pictures yet already changes are afoot as the Cornwall Railway 1859 route from Cornwall Junction to Cornwall Loop Junction was closed completely as from 16 January 1964, the track being removed five months later. As we shall later witness, the ironwork of Stonehouse Pool Viaduct was dismantled in the autumn of 1965 leaving the still extant masonry piers as a reminder of the structure. Common to both images is a clear view of a traffic-free Pennycomequick roundabout with, just to the right of the railway bridge, two names many will recall; Evans Stove Works and Skipper John's Fish and Chip Shop. *June 1966*

We move on four decades for our next visit to the Station Tower Block and, although the overall view is instantly recognisable, in the intervening 38 years there have been some subtle changes. To the far right the former GPO Sorting Office has gained an extension. Railway-wise only the Cornwall Loop of 1876 survives. The former line to Millbay which went off to the left was closed in June 1971 and was demolished in the autumn of 1974, the same year the track layout at Plymouth Station was re-organised. One noticeable factor is the reduction in the number of sets of points. The Locomotive Servicing Point was put out of use in 1966 but a couple of its sidings remained in use until 1975. A new landmark is the iron casting placed on the piers of the former Stonehouse Pool Viaduct, more of that later. Road-wise, Pennycomequick roundabout is by now getting less visible as the growth asserts itself. 37 308 in standard BR blue livery + 37 047 carrying the short-lived Mainline Freight blue livery arrive with 6C43 Carne Point (Fowey) to Tavistock Junction. An impressive rake of empty 'CDA' china clay wagons for Marsh Mills, this traffic would cease in 2008.
7 February 2004

And so to the present day where the most marked difference in the view is the incessant growth, which just about blocks the view of Pennycomequick roundabout and the former Royal Mail carpark. Railway-wise in all four pictures the main line heading west can be seen curving away to the top right to Devonport Junction which we shall visit (twice) in our travels. The Plymouth Panel Signal Box still keeps watch over the trains. 43026 + 43056 set off for the sea side with 1C76 0906 London Paddington-Newquay.
21 August 2013

THE CORNWALL LOOP FROM CENTRAL PARK

On a glorious summer evening, Class 42 'Warship' D867 'Zenith' approaches Plymouth Station with the 1755 Penzance-Bristol Temple Meads due in at 2008, the vantage point from Central Park offering a superb broadside view of the Cornwall Loop Triangle. The train is on the Cornwall Loop of 1876. Immediately behind the front of the train some milk tanks and a parcels van stand in the former Locomotive Servicing Point sidings, and point the way to the left hand arch under North Road West, the route of 1849 into Millbay. Look behind the fourth coach of the train and the right hand arch is the direct route from Millbay to Cornwall of 1859. Cornwall Junction was immediately to the other side of North Road West, and the course of the railway can be discerned into Millbay, the Duke of Cornwall Hotel forming a notable landmark. Other notable landmarks are the Hoe War Memorial and Smeaton's Tower to the far left; the spire of the Catholic Cathedral and the Millbay Grain Silo to the right, and in the foreground the stone pillars of the western low-level entrance to Central Park. *21 May 1970*

A return to the same vantage point shows a view which is now not quite so attractive. The notable landmarks from the top picture give us our bearings; the Hoe War Memorial and Smeaton's Tower on Plymouth Hoe are to the top left, the spire of the Catholic Cathedral is to the far right, but the Grain Silo is missing, having been demolished in 2008. The entrance to Central Park is still there. The young saplings of 1970 have grown to block out any decent view of the Cornwall Loop Triangle. The eagle-eyed will spot in exactly the same place as where D867 and train were photographed 153 382+150 239 working 2C56 1444 Penzance-Bristol Temple Meads. Fortunately, the houses behind still mark the spot, and we shall now stroll over to North Road West to view the scene. *22 March 2015*

In 1913 a locomotive servicing-point was created within the Cornwall Loop Triangle, accessed either from the Millbay Line or North Road. This was established to take pressure off both Laira Shed, and the bottleneck between North Road East and Lipson Junction.

Standing on the thoroughfare now known as North Road West and opposite the entrance to Patna Place, we see a view of the water crane and the simple coaling facilities provided here. A 'Hall' Class 4-6-0 is ready to leave for the station. To the left, the lines led to a turntable, a partial view of which will feature when we make our return journey from Millbay. The turntable was last used in 1963 and the Locomotive Servicing Point was out of use by 1966, although a couple of the sidings were retained mainly for engineering use until 1975. *August 1962*

We move the camera just a few yards to the right of the top picture to stand directly on the bridge spanning the double track curve of 1849 to Cornwall Junction and Millbay. The Locomotive Servicing Point was just to the left. By this time, the remaining rails south of the main line await demolition as Class 52 D1016 'Western Gladiator' is pictured taking the only route now left going west out of Plymouth Station with 1V72 Leeds-Penzance 'Cornishman'. *29 October 1973*

Taken in exactly the same spot as the centre picture, this is the view from North Road West today, with all traces of the railway in to Millbay and the Locomotive Servicing Point completely expunged. The ground levels of all former railway land have been raised to provide a small pleasure park and nature reserve, and anyone who did not know would have no clue whatsoever of any previous railway presence here. We shall return to the park in due course. *4 March 2015*

CORNWALL JUNCTION

As its name implies, this is where the Cornwall Railway of May 1859 made its physical junction with the South Devon Railway main line from Exeter and thus, until the advent of the Cornwall Loop in 1876, all trains from the east, bound for the west, were obliged to reverse at Millbay. We are standing in Archer Terrace looking at the double track from North Road to Millbay which had seen its last train only four months before. The substantial retaining wall is worthy of note. The route into Cornwall from here had been closed on 13 January 1964 and its track bed is to the left, passing beneath North Road West. The road bridge to the right is the one where the pictures on the previous page were taken from. Both bridges figure prominently in the view we have seen from Central Park. *3 October 1971*

The cutting was infilled many years ago and one would have no idea that there was once a railway junction beneath the pleasure park. The houses and buildings to the right in Patna Place remain as good landmarks to link both pictures, and that impressive stone wall is still there, most of it buried but the top of it remains as a natural boundary to the little green area. I wonder how many people realise just how deep in the ground that wall once extended. Is this really where once, in the shadow of the Catholic Cathedral, heavy boat trains pounded up the grade out of Millbay, and the sound of piston crank and hissing steam of the Great Western Saints and Stars made their own contribution to Holy Mass? It is a lovely thought! We shall call in again on the Cornwall Loop Triangle once our passage around Millbay is complete. *4 March 2015*

Turning around from the view of Cornwall Junction on the previous page and walking five yards down the road to the junction of Archer Terrace and Wyndham Street East, these pictures show the grandstand view, one could once enjoy here, of a railway installation. Common to both images are Harwell Street Carriage Shed – more of this later – and the houses of Harwell Street to the left, the main line descending at 1-in-61 to 1-in-65 from Cornwall Junction to Millbay with the former Belmont Diesel Depot to the right.

7029 'Clun Castle' runs past the carriage shed to collect its stock for the now legendary 1Z48 run to Paddington. This was, as far as I know, the last steam engine to be seen on the Millbay Lines, it was certainly the last one of this class. To the right is Belmont Diesel Depot, built on the site on Millbay Shed which had finally closed in 1931, and was in use from 1958 until 4 October 1964. It was mainly a DMU stabling, fuelling and inspection point, but was used by mainline diesel locomotives before Laira Diesel Depot came on stream in 1961. Its life was cut short by the Beeching cuts and falling local traffic which meant Laira Diesel Depot could absorb the work. *9 May 1964*

A splendid view from a great friend, the late Ron Lumber, supplied from the Dave Mitchell collection of Class 42 'Warship' D832 'Onslaught' growling nicely up the grade with the empty stock for 2C76 1640 Plymouth-Exeter St Davids. In the four years since 7029 was seen here there are a few subtle changes; the lifting of the two sidings in the immediate foreground, Belmont Diesel Depot, now disused and its rails used for empty stock stabling, while the skyline has a new feature – a block of high-rise flats. All that survives from this picture, railway-wise, is the engine, one of two of the class to enter preservation. *20 April 1968*

HARWELL STREET, THE CHANGED SCENE

Empty carriage stock stabling was transferred to Laira on 6 October 1969 and the line to the Docks closed completely on 30 June 1971, bringing the era of the railway serving Millbay to an end after 122 years. It's just over the three years since we saw D832 here, there is an air of dereliction and decay as the engineering train with its crane is parked up ready to commence track-lifting operations. Overall the view is still very much the same, the Belmont Diesel Depot Servicing Shed was still standing proud but the hustle and bustle has gone. No longer would any engine struggle up the grade to Cornwall Junction. *27 September 1971*

It is very hard to grasp that this is the scene at Harwell Street looking south just nine years after that busy scene with 7029. All the track has been lifted and Belmont Diesel Depot was already but a memory. For a few years the derelict railway site here stood as some sort of 'Berlin Wall' separating the modern Plymouth City Centre from the more rundown suburban streets of East Stonehouse. Although the land was sold off and the levels greatly altered, the City Council took its time to develop the site. As I recall, house building did not commence here until 1982. *November 1973*

This is the scene now on the corner where Archer Terrace meets Wyndham Street East. Further development is under way so the view will be lost for ever, unless one can purchase one of the new houses. There is not much more I can add, just to ponder how something so permanent like the railway at Harwell Street can vanish off the face of the earth, and this is the fate of all the railway lines which served Millbay and its Docks. *4 March 2015*

HARWELL STREET CARRIAGE SHED

Harwell Street Carriage Shed was a substantial structure with four lines of rail and stood directly opposite Hastings Street Methodist Church which is to the far right. On the main line to the left is the point where the Plymouth Panel Signal Box of November 1960 fringed onto Millbay Signal Box: the mechanical signal is the Millbay 'Down' home signal. The colour light on the opposite line is the first one on the panel in the 'Up' direction from Millbay and, until 1964, it would have indicated the route for either North Road Station or over Stonehouse Pool Viaduct, direct towards Cornwall. So, in the six years since the Panel had been established, there had been changes and of course many more were to come in a very short space of time. I do not know why I only took a close-up shot of the shed, late on a late summer's evening, but it does look very homely with the lights on. *July 1966*

An interior view of Harwell Street Carriage Shed showing how well constructed it was, with the steel roof and steel supports to the right, and a more conventional brick wall to the left. How I wish I could have had this taken down properly and relocated it on the Plym Valley Railway at Marsh Mills, instead of it being cut up and thrown into a contractor's lorry. Sadly, in 1974, the PVR was not even a blink of the eye. As we have seen, nothing at all remains of this fine structure, and to update the picture I would probably have to stand in somebody's kitchen, and that would be at a lower level as the bank has been removed for a housing estate. As far as I know, this is the only interior shot of the shed. Even at its end, it is spacious, with an atmosphere all of its own. *November 1974*

HARWELL STREET LOOKING NORTH

Demolition of the infrastructure of the Millbay line was well underway in the late autumn of 1974. This was the era before temporary, and often flimsy and unsightly, fencing was erected around any such site and also before the compulsory hard hat and fluorescent jacket was the order of the day. The contractor kindly allowed me to bring my little 100E car onto the former line. This was a quiet Sunday afternoon, and I claim to be the only person to have ridden from Cornwall Junction to the King Street Arch on a train and also driven the route in a private car! The view provides a last glimpse of the climb up to Cornwall Junction, where the bridge under North Road West, where once trains took the direct route to Cornwall, can be seen in the far background. To the left is Archer Terrace and Wyndham Street East, the corner where they met is the angle for the views we saw looking down on the Harwell Street complex. To the right is the carriage shed in its last throws of life, with Hastings Street Methodist Church and the houses of Harwell Street which, of course, still survive. It is interesting to study the heavy plant of the 1970s. *10 November 1974*

Such has been the transformation of the area, with levelling of the terrain and substantial housing development, that it is very difficult to get one's bearings railway-wise. Going from memory and working out the distance from both Archer Terrace and the houses of Harwell Street, this view, taken in Hetling Close, is just about in the correct place also taking into account the fact that the land here is now at a lower level. There is no indication a railway ever existed here. The scene does also give an indication of how the scene looking south from the meeting of Archer Terrace and Wyndham Street East, would be totally unrecognisable today. *22 March 2015*

THE KING STREET ARCH EASTERN SIDE

Continuing our somewhat detailed look at the railway from North Road to Millbay, we have moved on a few more yards down Harwell Street (on the far right) to where it met Western Approach, and standing in the central reservation of the latter we see the King Street Arch, carrying the railway over the thoroughfare of that name where this also joined Western Approach. This was not the prettiest sight in Plymouth. The stone wall leading to the more conventional embankment to the left was regarded as a barrier between the City Centre and the former borough of Stonehouse, a Plymouth 'Berlin Wall' and one which the City Fathers were eager to remove. Noticeable landmarks are the roof of the former Gaumont/Odeon cinema, and to the far left the bell tower of the Duke of Cornwall Hotel. *November 1974*

Walking up the central reservation of Western Approach in 2015 I thought not to be a wise idea, so using my intuition to obtain an updated shot of the present-day scene, the view is taken from the top deck of the number 83 bus! A few strange looks came from my fellow passengers, completely bemused by my explanation of updating a former railway view. The bend of the road and the tip of the roof of the Gaumont/Odeon cinema confirm the location, where the scene has been completely transformed by a combination of eradication of the railway infrastructure, changes to the road layout, provision of the footbridge and the Western Approach multi-storey carpark, the latter a venue we shall soon visit in our updating of the former Millbay railway scene. *5 May 2015*

Two pictures, both taken on a Sunday afternoon, which at first glance look remarkably similar. It is the same block of flats on the right; on the left it is the same corner of Cecil Street with its chemist shop, and on the far side of Western Approach, there is a glimpse of Frankfort Gate. What has changed is the central part of the two images where once stood the King Street Arch, demolished on 19 November 1974

The Chemist Shop is trading as EW Lake, MPS and next to it can be seen the sign for the Bulls Head pub, the 'Tivy' sign indicating this was a Starkey Knight & Ford House. On the masonry of the Arch stands an advertisement for Piccadilly Cigarettes – how politically incorrect that would be now! It all looks so permanent. *10 November 1974*

The flats to the right now have new railings and, where the arch once stood, the left hand side has become yet more housing. The Bulls Head saw its last licensee appointed in 1991 and in 1994 the licence was transferred to Tramps at Bretonside Bus Station. The corner of Cecil Street still has its chemist shop, now rebranded the King Street Pharmacy. In the background the footbridge from the Western Approach multi-storey carpark blocks most of the view of Frankfort Gate. *22 March 2015*

MILLBAY SIGNAL BOX

This classic example of a large GWR signal box stood above Western Approach. It was opened in June 1914 and closed on 14 December 1969. It had a 115-lever frame and was, from 26 November 1960, a fringe box to the Plymouth Panel. To its left stands the red brick cabin which was the original signal box, opened circa 1899. The doorway nearest the new signal box was the shunters cabin, the door in the middle was the Area Carriage & Wagon Foreman's Office and the far end of the building was the Carriage & Wagon store. It was as clerk to the Area Carriage & Wagon Foreman, Sam Cooper, that well known railway photographer Terry Nicholls started his railway career here in 1957, coming under the District Running & Maintenance Superintendent, Tommy Hall, who was based in Newton Abbot. Millbay was responsible for all the Carriage & Wagon examiners and repairers at Millbay as well as Plymouth North Road, Laira Yard, Tavistock Junction Yard, Plymouth Friary and Okehampton: a reminder of how the railway used to work. I am told there are many interesting stories about the red brick cabin but none of them are suitable to put in print! Terry moved to the Laira Locomotive Shed in January 1959 and promotion two years later took him to Bristol as clerk to the Divisional Locomotive Engineer. He moved to Bristol Control Office in 1980 and was relocated when this was moved to Swindon in 1984, retiring in 1997 as one of the Western Region Senior Controllers. So from a red brick cabin in Millbay to controlling the whole route from Paddington to Penzance, as well as to Worcester, Hereford, Bristol and South Wales is one of those stories which make railway lore. A notable landmark to the right of the signal box is the Plymouth Pannier Market then only seven years old, having been opened by the then Lord Mayor of Plymouth Councillor, Percy Washbourn, on 7 September 1959. I am pleased to report this fine building is still in daily use. The railway site here has been taken over by the Western Approach multi-storey carpark, and I thought a drab shot of one its floors would not really show anything of interest. *18 June 1966*

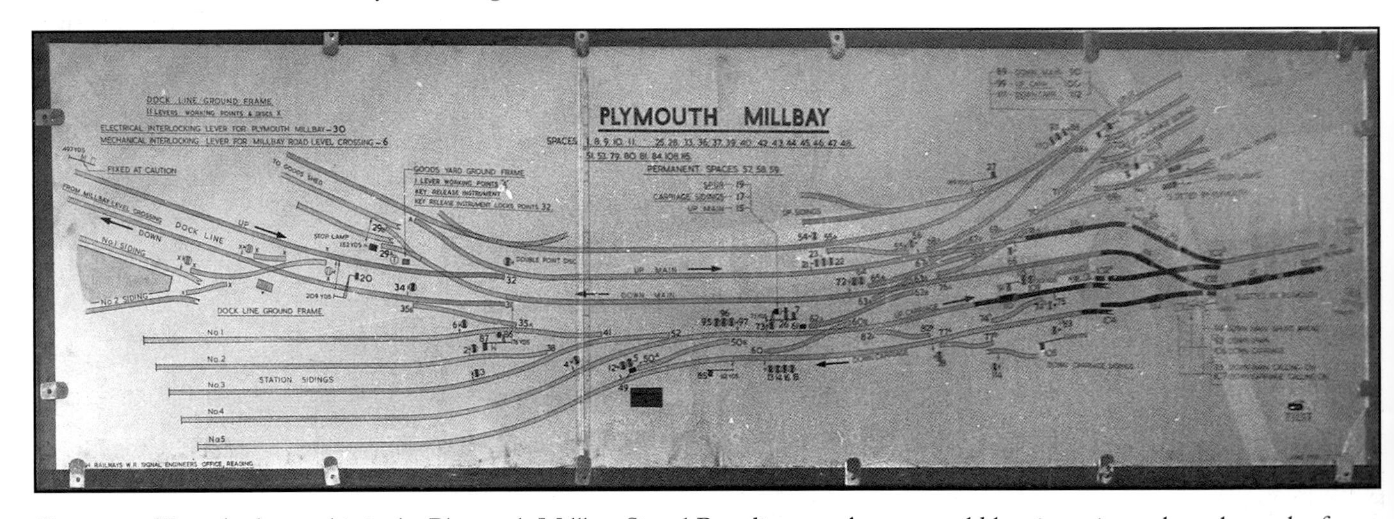

Courtesy of Ron Andrews, this is the Plymouth Millbay Signal Box diagram. A man would be given six weeks to learn the frame and the layout of such an installation. 1963

From high upon Western Approach, this is the impressive view from Millbay Signal Box looking north on a fine summer evening. To the far right we see Harwell Street and, on its corner, the Cardiff Arms which became the Town House. Then, moving left onto the railway, Harwell Street Carriage Shed can be seen opposite Archer Terrace and Wyndham Street East. Along the track we are looking back up the 1-in-61/65 descent from Cornwall Junction, with some impressive track-work on show. Notice how the points are arranged in order for any move to be made between the running lines and the various sidings. *July 1966*

The view from the signal box looking south was equally as impressive as that looking north. The five sets of lines to the left lead into the former passenger station opened on 4 April 1849. It was closed to passengers on 23 April 1941 due to bombing of the adjoining goods station and the need to thus use the passenger platforms for goods, which ceased here 20 June 1966. Empty carriage stock continued to be stabled here until this was removed to Laira on 6 October 1969. The two running lines next to the line of coaches are the route into the Docks closed on 30 June 1971 ending the railway era at Millbay. *July 1966*

The location is practically the same, now from the upper level of the Western Approach carpark. Other than the houses in Harwell Street to the right, there is no clue to any existence of the former railway and all that lovely point-work is but a memory. All that was once previously railway land seems to have been used to its maximum to cram in as much housing development as possible and, judging by the crane, building-work is still under way. *22 March 2015*

This is not a recent view, having been taken 16 years ago. The precise location is not now available as this part of the Western Approach carpark roof is covered in solar panels and public access is denied. If one could get the same picture today, I suspect it would look very similar with the Duke of Cornwall Hotel marking the spot, with the roof of the 1991-opened Plymouth Pavilions immediately to its right. The Telecom Building opened in 1982 is still extant but the Grain Silo was demolished in 2008. The picture serves to show how by the end of the last century Millbay Station and its rails had been consigned to oblivion. *October 1999*

THE UNION STREET ARCH, EASTERN SIDE

If there was one defining landmark of the railway system around Millbay it is the Union Street Arch, so named where the railway crossed Union Street at its junction with Western Approach. One wonders what traffic chaos, even in the day of the horse and cart, would have ensued if the original proposal here for a level crossing had been allowed. It was the Board of Trade's insistence on a bridge capable of taking locomotives that was one of the factors delaying the 1848 arrival at Laira reaching the Plymouth terminus. Union Street, as its name implies, is the thoroughfare which linked the separate borough of Plymouth with those of Stonehouse and Devonport. When built in 1812-1820 it was over reclaimed land, once a boggy marsh. Today it is part of the A374 road. Behind the Arch to the right the former Gaumont Cinema has become the Odeon; to the left note the small businesses which traded in the arches beneath the railway boundary wall. *November 1974*

The kerb of the bus bay and the former Odeon behind the tree confirm this is the precise location. To the right, Toys 'R' Us has replaced the former railway embankment and the Sweet Lemon Cafe. Where the railway arch once spanned the road, the pedestrian footbridge of the 1990s, linking the Pavilions and the Western Approach carpark stands, but at present is closed and has an uncertain future. The road layout has become a complex junction. There is sadly little to remind us of what was once a well-known and loved feature of the City Centre. *22 March 2015*

Like the former King Street Arch, a walk along where once it stood takes one from the hustle and bustle of the modern City Centre to the somewhat drab Stonehouse suburbs, a stark contrast still felt to this day. Look to the left of both pictures and there is The Two Trees, with, to its right, a bridge crossing Union Street. It is these that are different. The Union Street Arch was demolished in November 1974 and a similar fate likely awaits its 1990s replacement, the footbridge connecting Western Approach carpark and the Pavilions. Beyond we see the part of Union Street which forms the west end of Plymouth City Centre.

The road sign immediately in front of the arch really takes us back to the style of the 1970s, directing City Centre traffic straight on, Exeter and the A379 to Kingsbridge to turn right, and left for Saltash, Cornwall and the A386 to Tavistock. *10 November 1974*

The modern day road sign – who knows if people may one day look on this style with nostalgia – has moved forward a few yards and, due to the changes in the City road layout, Exeter-bound traffic is advised to turn left along with that bound for Cornwall on the A38 and Tavistock on the A386. Kingsbridge and the A379 no longer get a mention. City Centre traffic is still advised to go straight on and the litter bin in the top picture has made way for a new pole proclaiming parking restrictions, another feature of modern life. A noticeable addition to the skyline, behind the pub, is the Toys 'R' Us building and the Western Approach carpark built on the site of the former railway line. *22 March 2015*

THE UNION STREET ARCH, WEST SIDE

Cross over to the other side of the road and walk west a few yards, and the only real difference between the two images is the bridge, which crosses Union Street, and the bollards which have appeared alongside the new bus stop. On both sides of the road the buildings are the same, the background is dominated by the Civic Centre on Royal Parade.

How many first dates and romances started here at the Union Street Arch, how many trysts took place beneath the tracks above? This was a well known and popular spot for such meetings, although I never made use of the facility for such means! However, many others did and when the Arch went at the end of November 1974, so did a little piece of romantic Plymouth. The Odeon Cinema, formerly the Gaumont, was still open for business, or one could visit the Casino next door. *10 November 1974*

The Casino, below, has become a place for business design and print. The former Odeon after its time as a ballroom and a period of uncertainty is now being given a new lease of life as God TV where, in the digital age, the television station will broadcast to the world. I wonder if the new owners realise this is next to where Great Western Saints, and Sinners, pounded their way out of Millbay on God's wonderful railway? To the extreme right, next to what is now Club Jesters, and a well-known name in Plymouth, the Cabinet Supplies, still occupies the same premises. Sadly there is no reminder today of any former railway presence here. *22 March 2015*

THE BATH STREET ARCHES

Less well known, probably a case of out of sight and out of mind, were the Bath Street Arches. These were built into what was the west boundary wall of the Millbay Station complex, and as well as accommodating the odd small business, at one time they formed part of the once extensive stables for the Station. Local delivery and/or collection of traffic was handled by horse drawn carts until well after World War II. Real horse power for the railway was a common feature in many places all over the national system. There is no look of hustle and bustle here, just a sign of the neglect that had taken over the former station area. Look down the road and in the distance the Union Street Arch can be spotted. The other main feature of note is my 100E car. *10 November 1971*

Look down Bath Street, below, today and it is all change on both sides of the road, and it is the right hand side where this is more apparent. The Arches were demolished to make way for the building of the Pavilions opened in 1991. Further down the road the view of what was the Union Street Arch is somewhat obscured by the concrete of the Pavilions and there is a glimpse, if one looks carefully, of the green footbridge connecting the latter to the Western Approach carpark. When the Bath Street Arches were flattened, part of pre-war Plymouth was lost for ever and some more of the character of the City Centre was destroyed. To the left new buildings and a high wall add little character to the street. I did park my present car, my little Fiesta, as near as I could to where the 100E was parked to add a further degree of change between the two eras. Within a few years the City Council propose to further redevelop this area with the creation of a new boulevard stretching into the City Centre. *22 March 2015*

We return to the rails at the junction of the line into the Docks, looking towards Cornwall Junction, where there is a good landmark common to all three views, the Pannier Market.

The Branch Line Society Plymouth Area DMU Rail Tour has paused for a photographic stop on the up line from the Docks. The rear end blind of the DMU is displaying a somewhat optimistic destination as the lines to Chard had closed in September 1962. This was still the era in which when the train came to a halt, the doors were flung open and those who wished to alight just jumped down onto the track with not an orange jacket in sight. I think a thing called 'common sense' prevailed. To the left of the train is the former Goods Station, to its right the by now closed carriage sidings once part of the Passenger Station. One senses as this, the last passenger train on the Millbay system, pays a call that there is a feel of dereliction in the air. In the background the Pannier Market acts as a good landmark. *10 October 1970*

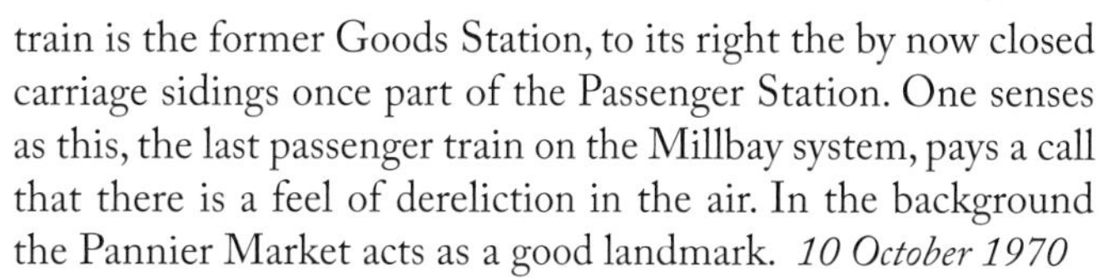

Millbay flattened. There is no trace of the railway at all but we have some familiar landmarks to line up the picture. Harwell Street shows up clearly in the background and to the far right is the Pannier Market. For a while this area was an eyesore at the bottom of the City Centre and did nothing to enhance its appearance. It would take the City Council a decade to rectify the situation. *April 1981*

The approach to Millbay is no longer an eyesore, the site having been transformed by the construction of the Pavilions, opened in 1991. Peering at the directions to the Ice Rink, this is just about the same spot. To the right the Pannier Market confirms we are indeed standing where the railway once approached Millbay Station. *22 March 2015*

MILLBAY STATION

Capturing this image required a walk to the front of the BLS Plymouth area Rail Tour for the view looking back towards the Docks with the station behind the train and the Duke of Cornwall Hotel dominating the scene. I am standing on the former Goods Station Sidings and there is an untidy look of decay as by this time the double track into the Docks remained the only operational line. The dull cloud and the haze do little to enhance what is a somewhat depressing scene, but this was my only chance to photograph a passenger train here. *10 October 1970*

Almost the same view point, with the Duke of Cornwall Hotel to give us our bearings. A temporary use of the Millbay Station site was made by the Plymouth Exhibition Centre housed in the inflatable Plymouth Air Domes who kindly agreed to display an ex British Railway built GWR design Large Prairie Tank – it was built in 1948 after Nationalisation – to be displayed from 13 May 1981 until March 1982. The engine was purchased from the Birmingham Railway Museum at Tyseley by a separate group with the intention of completing restoration for use on the then very embryonic Plym Valley Railway, moving to the Marsh Mills site when this became available just under a year later. To complete the 4160 story, it was removed to the West Somerset Railway in April 1990 to hasten restoration which was complete by the summer of 1993. Since then it has become a regular and popular part of their fleet. Who knows maybe it will return to Plymouth one day. As well as the cars of the period, take note of the Mount Pleasant Inn immediately to the left of the Duke of Cornwall. *March 1982*

There's not a lot to say about the present-day view overtaken by the Pavilions of 1991. The Duke of Cornwall and the Mount Pleasant both remain open for business. A glance to the right will explain why I could not get a satisfactory update for the top picture on the following page. I would probably have had to stand in the ice rink! *22 March 2015*

A third picture of the protracted (fortunately!) BLS Plymouth area Rail Tour photographic stop. Now I have crossed the tracks to stand in the October gloom for the view from the former carriage sidings, closed a year earlier. By now this is a rundown scene with an air of decay and dereliction. The angle is looking towards the Docks with the former passenger station to the left and the former goods station to the right. Spiller's Flour Mill and the Grain Silo are good landmarks in the Docks. We move down just past the rear of the train for a view looking in the other direction for the middle picture. *10 October 1970*

A view taken from the top of a signal of the PRC brake van special climbing out of the Docks double headed by D2177+D2178, we shall see the coming picture in due course. The rather drab goods station is to the left and to the right stands Dock Line Ground Frame, which gave access to the sidings where the engineer's stock was normally stabled and, in the carriage sidings we see Class 41 'Warship' D604 'Cossack' ready to leave with empty stock for Plymouth Station. Although from different angles one can garner how much the scene had changed in just four years. *18 June 1966*

The present-day view for the middle picture is about as drab as the former goods station. There is not a signal to stand on, just a carpark to stand in and work out the distance from the former level crossing. The result is another updated image which bears no resemblance whatsoever to the original. Yes, this is the same place. *12 August 2015*

MILLBAY STATION EXTERIOR VIEW

The fine exterior of Millbay Passenger Station, seen in the winter sunshine from the junction of Citadel Road and Millbay Road: I am just standing in the latter, the station situated on the former. I always considered this to be a somewhat elegant building in complete contrast to the interior of the station, thought by many to be rather drab and uninspiring. Across the road from the traffic bollard, the board tells us parking is 6d – six old pence – or two Shillings and amongst the adverts displayed is one for Maxwell House Coffee. Opposite the station we see the lampposts outside the Duke of Cornwall Hotel. A story related to me by one of its former employees is the complaint made by a gentleman, who arrived at Millbay Station sometime in the 1930s, alighted from the train and got into a taxi demanding to be taken to the Duke of Cornwall Hotel. The taxi driver duly obliged and after a 10 minute or so drive around Plymouth deposited his passenger and collected the fare. The gentleman, on waking the next morning, looked out of his bedroom window and the first thing he saw was Millbay Station! *25 December 1970*

Standing on the corner of Citadel Road and Millbay Road today, the view from the precise same spot shows that the Pavilions now occupies the site of the former station. Not much else to add really to this transformed scene. I suspect it costs rather more than 6d or two shillings (10 new pence) to park in the Pavilions carpark. *22 March 2015*

Having seen the south elevation of Millbay Station exterior on the previous page, we see the north-facing elevation which was a continuation of the building in the same style. To the north of the passenger station, as we have seen previously, the Docks Line dropped down the grade between this and the goods station and entered the Docks at Millbay Level Crossing where a signal box was provided. Railway-wise the view is looking towards Cornwall Junction. An Austin Cambridge car waits patiently on Millbay Road as Class 03 D2177 crosses the road on its way into the Docks to rescue D2178, which had failed with the PRC Brake Van Tour. Stabled on the former Fish Dock Sidings are engineering department vehicles and if memory serves me correct the leading one just behind D2177 is the tunnel-gauging van. Its 'Shunt with care' legend stands out well. Dock Line Ground Frame is in the background, the goods station was to the left. This is an iconic Plymouth area railway scene so fondly recalled by many to this day. *18 June 1966*

It is with a lump in my throat that I present the updated view. In my early years, sometimes on a Saturday afternoon or in the school holidays, my mother would take me to Millbay Crossing to see the gates open and close, and watch the trains coming and going from the Docks. Occasionally we were treated to an Ocean Liner Express forging its way out of the Docks at the start of its journey to London. Oh for a camera in those childhood days! Until the early 1960s there was a footbridge here, the upper view was taken from a very convenient signal. Neither exist today, so it is at ground level that I stand on the road which has replaced the railway and present, as best I can, a pinpoint update using the alignment of Millbay Road as the only link between the two images. Behind the trees stand the Pavilions. *22 March 2015*

MILLBAY LEVEL CROSSING

Recalling the 'going away' shot taken from this signal of the Rail Tour climbing up past Millbay Goods towards Dock Line Ground Frame; this is the 'coming' shot with D2177 and D2178 emerging from Millbay Docks, passing over the level crossing with a rather late-running Plymouth area Brake Van Tour. Top left in the background we see the Grain Silo and, behind the train, the cranes which once dominated West Quay. Looking towards the rear of the train, to the left is the Millbay Motor's garage with its yellow doors – take due note of this. On the right behind the signal box stands the railway warehouse. This will feature again as we progress in to the Docks. Here is another scene which many will fondly recall, it is so full of interest. *18 June 1966*

As we shall see in our tour around the Docks, there is very little evidence of the railway and the features it both passed and served that survive to tell the story. Here is one feature that does survive, the former Millbay Motor's Garage. I have this recorded in 1982 as a branch of National Tyre Service. Today it is no longer associated with the motor trade and is in use as Jobel's Bathrooms & Kitchens. The updated image is taken at a slightly lower level and a little to the left, standing more or less in front of where we saw the Tunnel-Gauging Van, this being the only suitable gap in the trees to obtain any decent view. The scene has changed considerably in the intervening years, with any trace of railway use totally eradicated. Behind the former garage we see not the Grain Silo but the Telecom Building of 1982, the railway warehouse is lost under the new road Isambard Brunel Way (hidden by the hoarding to the right) and the cranes of West Wharf have been replaced by the Brittany Ferries Terminal. Not quite such an interesting scene now. *12 August 2015*

MILLBAY LEVEL CROSSING 'UP' HOME SIGNAL

Once a train had passed over the level crossing into the Docks, it became under the control of the Docks foreman and the shunters, as there could be more than one train in the complex, serving the multiplicity of wharves, quays and the sidings that served the various businesses. The signal box is at the end of the fence and the garage, which is now Jobel Kitchen & Bathroom Centre, is to the right. The station is in the far background, as we move a few yards along the track towards the Docks. D2177 has been crossed over to the 'Up' line to rescue the failed Plymouth Railway Circle Brake Van Rail Tour, passing the level crossing signal box home signal which is to our left. Note the short distance to the inner home signal, immediately in front of the signal box, with the Millbay signal box 'Up' distant lower arm, a wonderful illustration of how the railway was signalled in those mechanical days. Also on the left is a very interesting Western Counties Brick Company lorry. *18 June 1966*

Like so much else of the Docks complex undergoing regeneration, this is an ever changing scene with the railway eradicated and new construction underway, so yet another view which will change in the immediate future. I can assure the reader that this is the same location, confirmed by the bend in the wall just to the immediate right of both images. It's amazing how, even with such great changes, sometimes one can still find a tiny clue to link past and present. *22 March 2015*

MILLBAY LEVEL CROSSING 'UP' DISTANT SIGNAL

So into the Docks and we arrive with a very interesting track layout to study. D2177 is standing on the curve which took the rails along East Quay towards the Ocean Terminal. To the left is the line which lead to Clyde Quay and the swing bridge and then circumnavigated the Inner Basin, a train having completed the circuit would then pass along the line in the foreground and reverse to exit the Docks. This is the route we shall take first in our tour of the former Docks system. Other than a diesel replacing a steam engine, I doubt if this was a scene that had changed in decades with the railway warehouse and the scrapyard. *18 June 1966*

One year and a decade since the last train passed through here and the scene is still recognisable with my little 100E car replacing D2177. Despite the line from Millbay Crossing becoming a road and some other associated changes and developments, enough of the track layout remains embedded in the tarmac to remind one of the former railway era here. To the left, a clearer view of the curved railway warehouse, to the right the then brand new Telecom Building. *August 1982*

The Telecom building remains as the only link between the two pictures above. All the railway lines and associated buildings have been swept away. That interesting little junction where, at the entrance to the Docks the trains once took their designated route, has been obliterated. Development work is under way here, so this is a view that will change either in the short or the long term. *22 March 2015*

TRINITY PIER FROM CLYDE QUAY

We start our circumnavigation of the Inner Basin by car rather than by train as, by 1982, the former rails along Clyde Quay had been replaced by a realigned road and, at that time, one was able to motor into parts of the Docks and drive along the former rail routes. From Clyde Quay we see a view of Trinity Pier, so named as its original use was for Trinity House purposes. It was once an intransient part of the Ocean Terminal and the former tenders were often berthed here. Bringing back memories of that era, alongside Trinity Pier is the PS Waverley, the last ocean-going paddle steamer in the world, on a rare visit to the City. Like the former Plymouth Tenders PS Waverley was a railway owned ship, built by the London & North Eastern Railway in 1946 (to replace a vessel of the same name lost in World War II) to work the railway operated steamer route from Craigendoran Pier, near Helensburgh through Loch Long to Arrochar. On nationalisation of the railways in 1948 all railway shipping in Scotland passed to the Caledonian Steam Packet Company which in time was merged with McBrayne's to become the still extant Caledonian MacBrayne. Withdrawn in 1973 due to increased running costs and heavy expenditure needed, she passed to the Paddle Steamer Preservation Society for a £1, and after much appealing for funds and much hard work, the rest, as they say, is history. On Trinity Pier with its lengthy Transit Shed, there is still much commercial activity as coastal shipping would continue to call here until circa 1988. *June 1982*

It is unlikely that the PS Waverley or any other commercial shipping will call again at Trinity Pier and one has to wonder if that historic Transit Shed will be sacrificed for yet more housing and/ or marina development. Fully restored it would be a fine monument to the heritage of the Docks but I suspect the developers would have other plans. The north side of the pier is still used by the MoD to ferry Royal Naval personnel out to sea. Notice in the top left background the warehouses of Millbay Ocean Terminal have been replaced by the Millbay Marina Development but the houses behind in West Hoe Road remain constant. Needless to say, I had to walk here for the updated shot as Clyde Quay is now inaccessible for road vehicles. *22 March 2015*

BY TRAIN ALONG CLYDE QUAY

By the miracle of my own personal time-machine – namely the camera – we can go back almost half a century and jump on a train here for a ride along Clyde Quay, so named for it was here that the Clyde Shipping Company vessels called until October 1966, thereafter it was only used by occasional trawlers. Along the quay the rails curved around the Transit Shed and other business premises here towards the swing bridge, which we can spot not too far beyond the engine. Beyond that the rails reached South Quay which we shall examine on the next page. The view is taken from the Plymouth Railway Circle Brake Van Tour, which would have been one of the very few to have ever conveyed passengers on this part of the Docks system. The trip around the inner basin was thus enjoyed by few people and offered me the opportunity to take some very rare railway photographs. *18 June 1966*

One of the very few pieces of track to survive in place in the Docks, a short section of the curve that leads to Clyde Quay. This and a convenient piece of raised ground to stand upon provide an unlikely location to update the original viewpoint from the goods brake van. Yes miracles do happen. Clyde Quay has changed out of all recognition, and it does not help the memory when this has already been dug up and altered more than once. Perhaps some people will ponder where these rails came from, what did they connect with? Moored up on West Wharf we see Ocean Majesty paying a call – the cruise ship and modern ferry terminal a world away from when this side of the Docks was part of the industrial side of the Port with cranes, noise, hustle and bustle, coal, dust, grain for the silo and much other traffic. Times have indeed changed here. *12 August 2015*

This is one of very few pictures ever taken from a train here, not from the carriage window but from the brake van verandah, and in its own way it is quite a nostalgic Docks scene with the cranes on South Quay to the right and the most northerly one of West Quay to the left. South Quay, with its 2x3-ton electric cranes, was where coal was handled: one of the coal bins is just visible to the right, the other hidden behind the stone wall. It was probably not the cleanest place to work in the Docks. I recall the train proceeded over the swing bridge at walking pace, I think there was a five-miles-per-hour restriction over the structure and, as the brake vans rumbled over, there was a very loud rattling noise. That noise is no longer to be heard here. The two levers in the immediate foreground are for the ground frame controlling the swing bridge, a full explanation of which will follow on the next page. *18 June 1966*

The lack of any structure crossing the entrance to the inner basin here today meant I had to stand a few yards back from the exact position of the 'Then' picture from the train. It is not possible to hover in mid air even for updated photography! Needless to say, the view has changed out of recognition with all the cranes, coal bins and former buildings swept away. Oil tanks now occupy part of South Quay, the background now dominated by the Britanny Ferries terminal and to the left the loading-ramp for vehicles on to the Ferry which berths by the former West Quay. One blessing perhaps is that the area is much cleaner these days without all the coal dust. *5 April 2015*

MILLBAY SWING BRIDGE FROM THE TRAIN

Looking back to the swing bridge from the rear of the Plymouth Railway Circle Brake Van Tour with Clyde Quay and its buildings behind, this was still very much a working quayside at the time. The swing bridge was part of a new line, built partly on reclaimed land, crossing the lock at the entrance to the inner basin and opened on 21 March 1945, this replacing the original swing bridge and lines constructed in 1902. Railway-wise, it was protected by two ground frames, one at either end, with the west ground frame clearly visible with its two levers on the left. To explain in simple terms, the line here was under the control of the shunter, not from any signal box. To prevent any rail movement being made with the swing bridge in the open position, i.e. to allow shipping to pass, a complicated system of Annett's keys (an Annett's key is used to unlock an item of signalling apparatus remote from a signal box) ensured the signals were at danger and the catch points at both ends open. A standard normal lower quadrant western region signal was provided at either end of the bridge, the one at the east end of the structure for west-bound trains clearly visible. Once the bridge was closed to shipping and reset for rail traffic, these were left in the 'off' position indicating that the structure was open for trains in either direction. *18 June 1966*

Not a precise update as this is the view from what was the eastern end of the swing bridge, taken more or less where we see the signal in the top picture. It is impossible to get to the swing bridge site on its western side due to security issues. Looking east along Clyde Quay, the changes speak for themselves. There is absolutely nothing left of that charming dock-area scene of the 1960s above and it is very hard to comprehend just how much this scene has altered. One useful landmark is just visible. The Civic Centre is almost blocked by the Telecom building, but one corner of it can just be spotted by the eagle-eyed to its right. One can only wonder if this is a scene which will change in the future. *22 March 2015*

If I had to choose an iconic scene of the railway in Millbay Docks, this would be the one. It is the only known colour picture of a train crossing the swing bridge over the entrance to the inner basin. D2178 with a string of brake vans on a Rail Tour was not the normal train to be seen here, this was always a freight-only line, but D2178 would have been seen here in its normal daily work. The signal in the 'off' position is controlled from the swing bridge west ground frame (as explained on the previous page) and indicates to any east-bound train that the swing bridge is open to rail traffic. To the right we can see the Jewsons Timber Yard on East Quay which we will visit in due course with, to the extreme right, Smeaton's Tower on Plymouth Hoe. To the far left there is another landmark: the Civic Centre on Royal Parade is just visible. *18 June 1966*

The view today can hardly be described as iconic as the west side of the former swing bridge is lost in the security area for boarding the cross channel ferry and is not easy to get to. Taking our bearings from the Civic Centre, just visible to the top left and partially hidden by the Telecom building of 1982, this view is not that far adrift. New construction has blown away any trace of Jewsons Timber Yard – and just about everything else, it has to be said. Any view of Smeaton's Tower from this angle is impossible. A totally transformed scene. Did Millbay really once have a swing bridge, one is tempted to ask? *2 August 2015*

THE ENGRAVING DOCK

The 454-foot-long Engraving Dock lay at the west end of Millbay Docks, in railway terms about 200 yards or so along from the swing bridge. Along with the rest of the docks, this was designed by IK Brunel. The entrance for shipping was from the inner basin adjacent to West Quay. The inner basin and the Engraving Dock opened in 1857, and Willoughby Bros Ltd (1857-1969) ship builders and repairers, were established here at the same time. Their large brick premises are to the top right. A welcome return visitor to Millbay was *La Duchesse de Normandie*. Built in 1931 for the Plymouth ocean traffic, the *Sir Richard Grenville* replaced a vessel of the same name and, with a break for Admiralty World War II service, served all her working railway owned life at Plymouth and became the last tender to be withdrawn in 1963. She was subsequently sold (and renamed) to Jersey Lines for service around the Channel Islands, departing Millbay for pastures new in January 1964. This was a welcome return to her old haunts for an overhaul, and also provided me with my only colour pictures of a Plymouth Tender in Millbay Docks – and, as it turned out, one of the few pictures ever taken on the floor of the Engraving Dock. Sadly Jersey Lines went in to administration at this time and the vessel did not return to the Channel Islands, but was sold for scrap and broken up. *November 1969*

Due to the contraction of the shipping repair business and the costs of repair, the Engraving Dock was closed and filled in 1973/74. Today the site is buried under the carpark for the Britanny Ferries Terminal and one would never know it had been there – which gave me the problem of how one gets an updated picture taken at the bottom of a filled in Dock. Well the answer is to stand at more or less its top and find a link. In the top picture look top left and there is a house with a window and to its right a flat roof. These can be picked out just to the left of the blue parking signs with a white van very thoughtfully parked up right under the aforesaid window with the flat roof just to its right. We shall see two further updated views from this carpark as we follow the railway around the Engraving Dock. *20 April 2015*

Walking around the Engraving Dock that bleak and cold November Sunday afternoon and seeing a former Plymouth tender in there brought back some happy memories. Besides their normal duties of attending liners in Plymouth Sound, the tenders doubled in summer as vessels for coastal cruising. These trips were extremely popular, mostly half-day excursions to Salcombe, Looe and Fowey and evening cruises around the Eddystone, a reef 14 miles distant from Plymouth with its famous lighthouse. A curious feature of these trips was seeing the tenders themselves dropping anchor and being served by much smaller tenders. A flotilla of small launches and rowing boats would appear. Due to their size, the vessels could not dock at Salcombe and Looe, and the port of Fowey was too concerned with china clay to be bothered about passengers. People had the option of paying a small additional fee to return by rail from either Looe or Fowey. Such marvellous variations of seeing the Cornish countryside have sadly been lost. In the summer of 1959 the tenders broke new ground when they operated cruises up the Hamoaze to view the floodlit Royal Albert Bridge, a subject to be discussed in due course. I well remember as a 12-year-old lad being on the first of these (June 25) when the tide was low and Sir Richard Hawkins scraped her bottom off Bull Point. I was fortunate to have enjoyed the Looe and Eddystone cruises, and often wish I had done the ultimate one: the August Bank Holiday Monday trip which covered Looe, Fowey, Dodman point and the Eddystone. What a day out that must have been! The last tender cruise was on 9 August 1963 to the most popular destination of all, the Eddystone. Organised by Plymouth Chamber of Commerce over 150 people were turned away. Such was the popularity of the tenders, and this was the effective end of coastal cruising from Plymouth.

The former *Sir Richard Grenville*, above, berthed in the Engraving Dock.
Same date for both images. November 1969

Below shows what it was what was like to be aboard a Plymouth Tender, standing on the deck in front of the wheelhouse, it was just as I remembered it.

MILLBAY DOCKS, THE WEST ENTRANCE

As our train journey around the Docks continues, the Engraving Dock is to the right but is hidden by the red brick shed. The tracks took a very sharp curve to the right at the start of the 180-degree turn to reach the North Quay. Here was located the western pedestrian and vehicle entrance to the Docks – the front of the train is hiding the gate – and on the other side of the wall we can spot the buildings in Admiralty Street, Stonehouse (we will come across another Admiralty Street when we reach Keyham), the most prominent of which is the Artillery Arms with a large advert for Devon Pale Ale on its wall and a military crest beneath. The green-coloured, flat-roofed building opposite – the roof was used as a landmark for the Engraving Dock pictures – has an interesting history: in the Eighteenth Century this was a fashionable hotel frequented by the gentry and in time became the Long Room Pub. The tree on the on the right mostly hides our first view of the Royal Marines Barracks. D2178 and its brake vans squeal around the curve on the PRC Rail Tour. *18 June 1966*

As we have seen, this part of the Docks complex is covered by a very large carpark for the Britanny Ferries Terminal, so it was a case of finding the right place to park the car. In effect, I am standing a few yards further forward and a little more to the left from the updated shot of the Engraving Dock. All traces of the railway have been swept away, but the boundary wall – and beyond it the Artillery Arms minus its Devon Pale advert, but still retaining the military crest, and the former Long Room (now a different colour) opposite – confirm that this is exactly the same spot. With the removal of the railway cabin and the tree, the south face of Stonehouse Barracks is more visible. The now heavily fenced gate at the western entrance to the Docks is not in normal use and stands directly opposite the Artillery Arms. *20 April 2015*

This is the next shot in the sequence and is taken more or less where D2178 is positioned in the picture at the top of the previous page. The train is going around the western end of the former Engraving Dock which has a rickety fence around it to prevent anyone falling in. To the right is a corner of Willoughby's well-built brick building. Behind the train is the unmistakable rear view of HM Royal Marine Barracks in Durnford Street (which dates from 1756 with additions in the 1790s and 1800s) and is still in use as the headquarters of 3 Commando Brigade. This is the oldest barracks that is not part of a fortification still in use in the country today, although there is now a question over its future. Going back to 1966, I just wonder what the health and safety brigade of today would make of a train of wooden break vans undertaking a tour of a Dockland railway system passing by a dry dock with very little protection. We all survived to tell the tale. D2178 is rounding the Engraving Dock. *18 June 1966*

Here we are 49 years later in the same place with Stonehouse Barracks, which has barely altered. In contrast, just about everything else has. The railway has been eradicated, the Engraving Dock filled in, Willoughby's red-brick building replaced by a bland modern structure and we continue our detailed examination of the carpark for the Brittany Ferries Terminal. Not only has Millbay Docks lost its railway heritage, it has lost its maritime heritage as well. The western end of the complex is now a roll-on-roll-off ferry terminal, the east side is either a Marina or what I would call 'Yuppie Land' with the bit in the middle of the Docks fenced off as some sort of secure 'no-man's land'. Once one could go round the inner basin in a circle on a train, and I was one of the privileged few who made the journey. *20 April 2015*

MILLBAY DOCKS, WEST QUAY SIDINGS

Having negotiated the west end of the Engraving Dock, the tracks then took a lovely 'S'-bend curve before the final right turn to reach the North Quay. In a way it is the sort of scene which typifies the former Dockland Railways, once so numerous with their sharp curves, sidings and various premises. Some wagons are parked up in the West Quay sidings, probably with traffic for Willoughby's and maybe the flour mill, or even possibly for Robert Daniel. I am reliably informed that local entrepreneur Robert Daniel, who went on to become Chairman of Plymouth Argyle, started his business in the building on the left, opposite the wagons and mostly hidden by the tree. Beyond the wagons the line takes a very sharp right turn to complete the 180-degree turn and reach the straight rails of the North Quay. D2178 and its brake vans slowly pass round the curves next to the cobbled road. *18 June 1966*

Our detailed tour of the Brittany Ferries carpark now concludes, standing at its north end. Look to the left and the road outside the carpark fence follows the curve of the cobbles which we saw beside D2178 and its brake vans in the top picture. Easily recognisable are some of the houses and buildings in the background on Millbay Road – they are more colourful these days – which confirm this is the same location. Like elsewhere in the Docks, no trace whatsoever remains of the railway and its associated structures, likewise of Mr Daniels and his business. West Quay itself has been lost with the infilling of that part of the Inner Basin. I suspect many motorists parking their cars, passengers joining the ferry and indeed anyone else who has cause to venture this way would not bat an eyelid at the bland carpark that exists today. Who would realise what history is contained in and under such a concentrated space? *20 April 2015*

The Plymouth Railway Circle Brake Van Tour has come round the curve from the West Quay to a busy dockland scene on the western end of North Quay, not to be confused with North Quay in Sutton Harbour. North Quay had 4x3-ton coastal shipping cranes set on their own wide-gage tracks; to the right are substantial stone-built transit sheds and rails set in the road, which unlike their counterparts on the Barbican have vanished without trace. This was what dockland railways were like. They were built not for passengers but for freight and cargo. We see a couple of ships berthed, nearest the train is the 'Robert Dundas', take note in particular, to its immediate right between the crane the inverted 'V'-shaped roof, of a building in Stonehouse Barracks whose roof is just visible behind. Make a note of these for the next picture. *18 June 1966*

To find a landmark these days to link two pictures in Millbay Docks is an achievement. Look to the right of the Dock café-bar-restaurant and that same building with the inverted 'V'-shaped roof in Stonehouse Barracks survives with its roof now more visible. These give us our bearings and prove this is the identical viewpoint. The changes here are substantial. Moving from left to right, note land reclamation in the harbour, the construction of the Dock Café, the road to serve the Britanny Ferries terminal and the transit sheds obliterated to be taken over by the check-in lanes for cars boarding the cross channel ferry. *12 August 2015*

MILLBAY DOCKS, THE WAY THINGS WERE

A couple of magnificent pictures taken by the late Paul Townsend, a great shipping enthusiast and photographer, supplied from the AC/BM Collection.

On a wonderfully calm October afternoon, looking from South Quay we see berthed on North Quay the *Annette Dania* (698 tons), built in 1969 and worked until about September 2007, with to the left, the warehouse bearing a Robert Daniel Cash 'N' Carry sign. To the right of this are the still extant houses in Millbay Road and the scene is completed by another great former local landmark, Spiller's Flour Mill, showing what a magnificent structure this really was. *25 October 1972*

The photographer has moved a few yards to the right onto Glasgow Wharf for this fine shot of the Stadt Brake, built in 1962 and later rechristened the Delos and then River Rose. This is the inner basin and the working commercial dock I remember so well. The background is dominated by (working from left to right) the still extant houses in Millbay Road, Spiller's Flour Mill and Pickford's Warehouse. This was a truly impressive skyline and it is hard to believe that it has largely vanished. *3 October 1973*

Standing on what remains of Glasgow Wharf today, I was able to use the houses in Millbay Road on the left to link the two images. How North Quay has changed, as we saw with D2178 under the cranes by the warehouses, not only has the background altered so much with the Flour Mill and Pickford's Warehouse demolished in 1998, the quayside itself has been realigned with more reclamation. Where once commercial shipping loaded and unloaded its cargo, there is now the King Point Marina, and a skyline of iconic commercial buildings has been replaced by bland modern apartment buildings. Millbay really has lost its soul. *5 April 2015*

THE MILLBAY METRO

A very rare visitor to Millbay Docks was this London Transport Underground stock. This is 1996 Jubilee Line stock and this particular specimen is a Driving Motorcar. The first six train sets were manufactured in Alstom's Barcelona factory, and the bodies shipped to the UK via the Santander-Plymouth Ferry; they were then taken on by road to the Midlands. The rest were built in Washwood Heath, Birmingham, so this must be one of number 96001-96006. So the next time one is in London and riding around on the Jubilee Line, it is quite possible your train, or part of it, started its life in England on North Quay, Millbay Docks. To the best of my knowledge, this is the only occasion London Underground carriages have been seen in Plymouth. *6 November 1996*

We shall now take an imaginary trip around the curve from North Quay to East Quay back to the railway dock entrance to complete our survey of the Millbay system.

ON TO THE EAST QUAY

Having made the circular journey around the inner basin, we are now back where we entered the complex by rail just down the line from Millbay Level Crossing. Looking south from there, we have a wonderful view of D2177 heading light engine along East Quay, which was constructed in the late 1840s. To the left is the extensive yard of Jewson's Timber Merchants, who received seaborne soft woods in a rough state, and cut and distributed them according to customer requirement. This well-known national firm still trades from two locations in the City, but sadly not for many years on the East Quay at Millbay. In the distance is the Ocean Terminal with, on the right, its three Piers; Trinity, Princess Royal and Millbay. When one mentions Millbay Docks, this part is probably the most recalled because here was the glamour of the Ocean Liner traffic and the specials to London. The full story has been told elsewhere and is well beyond the scope of this book, I can only bring you what I was able to see and record. *18 June 1966*

It is a very different view now looking south along East Quay. Today one stands in Soap Street, the name reflecting that, prior to the era of Jewson's and the timber yard, this was the site of the Millbay Soap Works, established as far as I know circa 1830. This part of Millbay was then ripe with large noisy and smoky industrial buildings, a stark contrast to the modern clean and white Quadrant Quay development that now occupies the site. All traces of the railway and former industry here have been eradicated, and instead of seeing the Ocean Terminal in the distance, one sees the Millbay Marina Village. However, there is a very good common link to both pictures proving they are taken from the same spot. Look down the quay and on the right one can spot Trinity Pier and the east end of its Transit Shed. *8 August 2015*

MILLBAY EAST QUAY FROM THE CARRIAGE WINDOW

I suspect that very few pictures were taken from the carriage window going along East Quay. Here are a couple of mine taken from the Branch Line Society Plymouth Area Rail Tour in October 1970. As far as I know this was the only Diesel Multiple Unit to ever traverse the line into the Ocean Terminal, and the very last passenger train to be seen here. So again, some rare material to enjoy.

Looking down the line from the railway entrance to the Docks along East Quay to the Ocean Terminal with Trinity Pier to the right, and Princess Royal and Millbay Piers behind. To the immediate left is a good supply of wood for Jewson's Timber Yard. A rare chance to study the track layout here: notice the check-rails laid in between the running rails to prevent derailments whilst running in a street and dockland environment. *10 October 1970*

We change sides and look the other way from Trinity Pier back along the East Quay to the point where the railway entered the Docks. The already explored and now much changed Clyde Quay is to the left, Jewson's timber is to the right. One gains the impression of this being very much a working port. *10 October 1970*

Needless to say I have no chance to do an update from the carriage window, so it is a case of taking a gentle stroll along the former East Quay and working out the nearest angle available to the original. The bend of the harbour wall on the left confirms the location. This is just as well as there is little else to link the two images. Soap Street of the Quadrant development has replaced Jewson's Yard. Clyde Quay to the left and just about everything else we can see in the 1970 picture has been rebuilt or redeveloped. The temporary fencing indicates construction work is still on going, so this is a view that could change in the short and long term. *2 August 2015*

A third view from the carriage window of the train approaching the Ocean Terminal with Trinity Pier to the immediate right and just behind it is Princess Royal Pier and behind that is the distinctive look of Millbay Pier with its canopy and the Dock Offices. Some period cars add interest to the view. *10 October 1970*

Arrival at the stop-blocks with a closer view of Millbay Pier and its canopy. And so now to tell a story of bribery and corruption. The rails within the Docks beyond Millbay Crossing had passed to the Docks Board in 1963. One condition they stated on accepting this Rail Tour was that no one would be allowed to alight from the train except for operational purposes. The District Inspector accompanying the train was my fellow colleague and great friend Edgar Whitear who was an avid stamp collector. Now father's sister, Aunty Gubbie, had emigrated to South Africa after she married Bill Northcott in the 1930s, and she provided plenty of that country's stamps for my father's collection with lots of duplicates. I do not recall the exact specimen but, as the train came along the East Quay, I showed Edgar a very rare high-value Edward VIII South African stamp. His eyes popped out of his head and I said if I was allowed out of the train as part of the operational crew – to check the tail-light would be the official excuse – he could put the stamp in his wallet and take it home. Thus my operational duties yielded these precious pictures, the only known colour ones of a train in the Ocean Terminal. Bribery and corruption can be put to good use at times! *10 October 1970*

This was the first passenger train to have been seen in the Ocean Terminal for seven years and it would also prove to be the last. There was not much time for my 'operational duties', so photography had to be thick and fast. Viewed from Trinity Pier, the Ocean Terminal certainly by this time had a run-down appearance, amplified by the rather dilapidated canopy to the left of the DMU. Industrial use of the site continued within the fine warehouses, and we can spot the premises of J Collingridge with its ready supply of wooden pallets. *10 October 1970*

An almost similar viewpoint a dozen years later; look to the background for the major change, the demolition of the covered walkway on Millbay Pier. Otherwise, with the exception of the removal of some of the railway track, this light-industrial scene looks pretty similar. Messrs J Collingridge are still doing business and the warehouses still stand proud. Demolition of the former station canopy has given an enhanced view of the former Pier Hotel now dealing with matters of trade rather than guests. A covering present-day view will follow on the next page. *March 1982*

MILLBAY OCEAN TERMINAL

A closer view of the DMU standing in the former Ocean Terminal. It is included because pictures of passenger trains here are so rare. The era of the Ocean Liner traffic here was to last for just under a century. It really took off in the 1870s, when steamship operators realised that if Trans-Atlantic ships from the New World called in at Plymouth, to deposit both mail and passengers, they would save a day on the journey to Southampton. The heyday was no doubt in the 1930s and after a short post-Second World War surge a new terminal here was opened in 1952. When the first Trans-Atlantic jet took off in September 1958, the writing was on the wall for the Ocean Liner traffic at Plymouth. Full boat-trains finished when the French Line ceased to call in 1961. Then, for a couple of years, occasional portions attached to mainline trains at Plymouth were run as required, until the traffic ceased with the last liner calling on 19 October 1963. To the left we see the somewhat battered buildings of the Ocean Terminal and some of the fine warehouses found here; these buildings were demolished in 1988. Behind the train we get a closer view of the covered way of Millbay Pier. How many passengers and bags of mail had once passed beneath that canopy I wonder? To the right is the Princess Royal Pier. *10 October 1970*

Believe it or not this is the same location today, the updated shot taken a few feet further back from the original image showing how the railway, the former Ocean Terminal buildings and the warehouses have been totally eradicated along with any building that stood on Millbay Pier. The sloping pontoon bridge – where the updated picture on the next page is taken from – rests on what remains of the Princess Royal Pier providing access to the pleasure boat berths. The whole topography of the location has completely changed. There is no connection in this view with the past whatsoever; not the first time we have come across such a situation in our tour around Millbay. One small part of the Ocean Terminal survives as some of the interior bar fittings which were presented to the Plym Valley Railway and are presently in store at their Marsh Mills base. *15 March 2015*

The tail light is being reset to red as the train crew change ends for the journey back to Millbay Level Crossing, and thence back to the main line. I had become part of the team to check that we had a red light on the rear for the return run along the line, so I had to attend to this end of the train as well! To the right are the buildings and warehouses of the Ocean Terminal, with a Securicor van doing its rounds; the railway line is set by the dockland cobbles. To the immediate left is the east end of Princess Royal Pier with the Transit Shed on Trinity Pier behind. Note the Morris Traveller and the Hillman Husky parked up. We also have a good view looking north straight along the East Quay. This was the last passenger train to be seen here, and no more were to visit as total closure would come only eight months later. *10 October 1970*

The former Ocean Terminal was extensively redeveloped in the early 1990s as the Millbay Marine Village and the original viewpoint is now lost under the housing (see top right). The updated view is taken a couple of yards forward and to the left from the remains of Princess Royal Pier with the Transit Shed on Trinity Pier marking the spot. Where the tenders once berthed, the moorings have been altered for the needs of pleasure craft. Thus a much changed view here, but at least the Transit Shed on Trinity Pier provides a common link, in contrast to the view down East Quay which has altered beyond recognition with the Quadrant Quay buildings dominating the scene. It is hard to realise that this peaceful looking Marina was once a very busy interchange point for ocean liner passengers and mail for a fast train to London. *15 March 2015*

MILLBAY PIER

We are looking east along Millbay Pier towards the former Ocean Terminal. Even though it had been just under 12 years since the last train had called, other than for the removal of the canopy, for Ocean Liner passengers, little had really changed. In the far right background we see the unique customs building, to the left the former Pier Hotel, still in commercial use, with the warehouses alongside, in front of them the remains of Princess Royal Pier. To the left, the skyline is dominated by the Mayflower Post House Hotel, (later the Quality Hotel) on Plymouth Hoe, which opened in 1970, closed in 2013 and, after a series of arson attacks, was demolished in July 2016. The Onward Mariner trawler from Fleetwood is tied up alongside and the whole area still has that busy look about it. On Millbay Pier the rails of the baggage railway, which also carried the mobile steam crane, are still in place, almost waiting for the next tender to arrive. *March 1982*

Such has been the transformation of this part of the Docks, it is impossible, at present, to access Millbay Pier and even if one could there would be little to see as everything has been swept away. The only possible updated view is from back a few yards through a gap in the fence in the appropriately named Great Western Road, where the background of East Stonehouse and the Long Room confirm the location. To the immediate right the Customs building survives due to its unique architecture, the only physical reminder of the ocean traffic era. At the time of writing, planning consent has been given for a very futuristic Dubai-style development on Millbay Pier, so this is yet another scene which will change, and probably very dramatically. Now, after our extensive look at Millbay Docks and its railways, it is time to return to the main line. 22 March 2015

Having been in and out of Millbay, we reverse for the journey west and return to the main line to revisit the Cornwall Loop as seen from North Road West.

In the immediate foreground we see part of the turntable of the Locomotive Servicing Point, last used in 1963.To the left is Stonehouse Pool Viaduct, the route of the Cornwall Railway out of the City opened on 4 May 1859 and closed on 16 January 1964. Sadly demolition work has just commenced. Crossing the 176-yard-long Cornwall Loop Viaduct is Class 43 Warship D844 Spartan with the 'Up' Cornishman on its way from Penzance to Leeds. *4 November 1965*

The former Locomotive Servicing Point and indeed all land to the south of both viaducts was subsequently raised and levelled to create a small green open space. The higher level of the land is well marked as we see 50 032+50 001 double head the 1345 Penzance-Plymouth local train. There was no operational need for this train to be lavished with such generous motive power; it was just a convenient way of working a spare engine back from Penzance. To the left the masonry piers of Stonehouse Pool Viaduct stand as a reminder of the original route to the west. The Locomotive Service Point is by now a distant memory, but the streets and houses behind the train look much the same. *5 October 1981*

This is the same view today, now a pleasant park and nature reserve. We can see enough of the background houses to confirm that this is the same view, where one can hear the trains on the main line, but find it hard to catch a glimpse of them. We shall return for a closer look at the Cornwall Loop when we trace our steps back in to Plymouth by way of the SR main line. *4 March 2015*

STONEHOUSE POOL VIADUCT FROM VICTORIA PARK

When the railways were constructed in this area, the local scene and topography were very different from that of today. Stonehouse Creek extended well inland and at high tide the sea reached the Mill Bridge above which was Stonehouse Mill Pond, this extending to the wharf at Pennycomequick. The creek was infilled to celebrate the 60th year of the reign of Queen Victoria and created the Victoria Park we know so well today. When the Cornwall Railway built their viaduct here for the line out of Millbay it crossed water, hence the name Stonehouse Pool Viaduct. At 321 feet in length and a maximum height of 57 feet, the original wooden structure was notable for a couple of reasons. Firstly it was the only one built for the Cornwall Railway to take double broad-gauge track. Secondly, other than Penzance – which was replaced by an embankment built into the beach at Long Rock – it was the last timber viaduct to be replaced on the main line west of Plymouth. The new structure opened in 1908 and remained in use until January 1964.

One lady and her dog watch from the park as Class 35 'Hymek' D7000 passes over Cornwall Loop Viaduct with the 0830 Paddington-Penzance. The 'Hymek'-Class diesels were not an everyday sight west of Plymouth and this was an unexpected bonus. Stonehouse Pool Viaduct stands proudly in front. *30 October 1969*

The view from the park looks very similar today, obvious factors being the growth, some of which partially hides the view of the station tower block, and the metal structure which rests on the piers of the disused viaduct. More of that later. 43 023 leads with 43 078 on the rear over Cornwall Loop Viaduct with 1C82 1206 London Paddington-Penzance. Victoria Park is still a nice place to sit and watch the world and the trains go by. *4 March 2015*

A further angle of the viaduct taken from the east end of Victoria Park, Cornwall Junction would be to the right. The original viaduct was a timber structure with five sets of timber fans built onto a small masonry base to support the arches. These were replaced by nine brick piers to carry the lattice-steel girders and super structure, five of which were built on the original masonry plinths of the timber structures and these can be spotted today quite easily from a simple stroll in the park near the viaduct. The steam crane is at work as demolition of the metalwork is under way, providing a last look at something on the viaduct from the park. *30 October 1965*

Using the layout of the park paths, the view is instantly recognisable. Other than ironwork removal and growth, the main change is the steel sculpture named Moor by local artist Richard Deacon CBE, placed on the redundant piers of Stonehouse Pool Viaduct at the time of the Millennium. This is supposed to represent the spirit of Brunel and his structures, but with due respect to its creator, the message is lost on me. Perhaps some explanatory plaque would be of use. Take your bearings from the two cabins standing at the base of the piers, and immediately to their left one can see one of the masonry stubs which supported the timber fans for the original viaduct. *4 March 2015*

DEVONPORT JUNCTION, WINGFIELD VILLAS HALT

A picture that kills two birds with one stone; taken from 1A94 1400 Penzance-Paddington express, the idea is to show Devonport Junction from the train, where the former SR route from Devonport Kings Road, on the right, joined the Cornwall main line. It also marks the site of one of the shortest-lived stations in Plymouth – Wingfield Villas Halt – whose platforms lay on the GWR line a few yards west of the junction. Opened as part of the rail-motor suburban boom on 1 June 1904, its life was short and it closed in June 1921. As far as I know, there is no known photograph of the station. *March 1966*

With the Southern main line in the foreground and about to pass the Devonport Junction 'Up' home signal, a mid morning 'sandwich train' from Saltash to Plymouth, probably the 1018, passes through. The view is taken from the south end of the road bridge which crosses both lines of route here. Interestingly, the train is formed with the middle coach being one of the twelve Brake/3rd-class compartment stock vehicles built in the 1930s and converted for auto working in 1954-55. They were numbered W245W to W256W and transferred to the West Country from South Wales in 1958. These were not commonplace on the Saltash workings due to capacity issues, venturing more out on to the Tavistock Branch. *AC/BM Collection, 18 May 1960*

The same angle from the south end of the road bridge today reveals little of railway or any other interest. As we shall see later when we return to this point by the SR main line, the latter has been obliterated and filled in, altering the topography of the location. The roof of the block of flats to the extreme left of the centre picture can just be glimpsed through the trees. This is a junction no more, with just the route to Cornwall remaining. Similar to standing in North Road West, one can hear the trains here and not see much of them. *4 March 2015*

The Cornwall Main Line climbs away from Devonport Junction up the short but steep 1-in-59 of Devonport Bank, starting to gain height to cross the Tamar at Saltash. With the Southern metals in the foreground, this is a very rare shot of a Diesel Multiple Unit conveying milk tanks as tail traffic as 2C74 0945 Plymouth-Saltash wends its way up the hill. Due to the cramped and difficult operating layout at Saltash – as we shall see in due course – return empty milk tanks from London for Saltash were dropped off at Plymouth and worked forward locally. It would have been impractical for the actual milk empties train to have called at Saltash with all the necessary shunting. On arrival at Saltash, the DMU would run around the milk tanks in the 'Down' platform, just like an engine would, and then propel them out towards Coombe Viaduct to reverse on the crossover to the 'Up' main line into the station, with then a further reversal into the goods yard, which we shall see illustrated in due course. The DMU with milk tanks berthed would then return as the 1020 passenger train to Plymouth. *7 March 1968*

With all traces of the Southern rails long since gone and heavy growth restricting the view, the updated image has had to be taken a little further to the right of the top picture. This is the scene today with what passes as the 'Cornish Riviera Express' 1006 London Paddington-Penzance climbing away from Devonport Junction on its way west. We shall return to Devonport Junction on our return trip along the former Southern main line in due course. *4 March 2015*

DEVONPORT ALBERT ROAD

It is just 62 chains from Devonport Junction up the 1-in-59 ruling gradient of Devonport Bank to its summit at the east end of Devonport Albert Road Station where the railway passes under the Havelock Terrace Road Bridge, our next vantage point.

One of the rather more camera-shy Class 52s D1007 Western Talisman passes by with 1C55 1230 London Paddington-Penzance booked to depart Plymouth at 1634. There are a couple of other points of interest to mention. Crossing the Devonport Road overbridge is one of the first of the one man operated 'Atlantean' double-decker buses, recently introduced by Plymouth Corporation Transport, running on the former route 1: City Centre-Peverell-Milehouse-Devonport-City Centre circular. The start of the era when the profession of bus conductor became a threatened – and then almost extinct – species. To the right of the train is the trailing siding which led the short distance to the former Goods Yard. This was closed to commercial traffic in 1957 to become a small Engineering Depot, which, I recall, housed the Signal & Telegraph Department. This siding was taken out of use on 20 September 1970 and, like the former Goods Yard, has vanished without trace. *2 June 1970*

The view is now heavily overgrown, enough of the platform and the Devonport Road overbridge remains to confirm the location, which does afford a good place to watch a steam-hauled special heading for Cornwall. 'Battle of Britain' Class 34067 'Tangmere' tops Devonport Bank with 1Z37 0850 Bristol Temple Meads-Par 'Royal Duchy'. Only a handful of these engines passed through here in the steam era. They were of course far more familiar just down the road at the Southern Kings Road Station, which we shall visit in due course. *2 August 2015*

The view is of the rather cramped but substantial station by which the GWR served the Borough of Devonport – proudly independent until its forced marriage with Stonehouse and Plymouth in November 1914 to form the united town that, in time, became the City of Plymouth we know today. It was not as grand as its southern neighbour Devonport Kings Road, which was at the other end of Exmouth Road and which we will examine in due course. We are looking west from the Havelock Terrace overbridge and down on the station, which was built partly in a cutting. Top right is the rear of St Michael's Church. The former signal box was closed on 26 November 1960, when the area was placed under the control of the Plymouth Panel Signal Box, behind which there is a prominent row of advertising hoardings in Exmouth Road and the entrance to the 125-yard Devonport Tunnel. It all looks so permanent. *22 September 1969*

It is very hard to grasp that there is only a period of six weeks between these two images, for this was a period when the word 'rationalisation' came to the fore and it was a depressing time of the railway ridding itself of as many liabilities and redundant buildings as it could. Devonport Albert Road was a major casualty. A lower angle from the station footbridge shows that the demolition gang have done their worst as Class 52 'Western' D1016 'Western Gladiator' emerges from the tunnel with, despite the wrong head code, 1A16 0915 Penzance-London Paddington. It could be said the station almost disappeared overnight. *8 November 1969*

DEVONPORT ALBERT ROAD

Still looking at the west-bound view from the Havelock Terrace overbridge and at first glance not a lot seems to have changed since the carnage of the autumn 1969 demolition. The former signal box has been demolished, the GWR-type station sign on the 'Up' (right hand) platform has been removed and of the original station, only the footway of the once covered footbridge remains. Above the tunnel the former Kimber's Garage, now Sandwell's Car Care Centre, is prominent. The advertising hoardings are no more. They would have been partially obscured by the trees which have grown in the intervening years. Possibly the biggest change is off the rails, the background now dominated by the Frigate Complex in the Dockyard, completed in 1977. An unidentified HST passes by, bound for Penzance. *November 1982*

So to the present day. The worn-out original footbridge was replaced in 2008 by the present structure. A combination of housing development and growth block any view of Exmouth Road, Kimber's Garage, and pretty much everything else. Opened on 4 May 1859 with the Cornwall Railway from Millbay to Truro, this is the oldest of all the stations, within the City, still open for passenger traffic. By a quirk of railway history, it predates the present Plymouth Station by 18 years. The suffix 'Albert Road' was added by British Railways on 26 September 1949, but dropped from 6 May 1968 when the service to the former Southern main line became the Gunnislake Branch. Served by the Plymouth-Gunnislake service and some mainline local trains, at least Devonport still has a station. 43015 leads with 43035 out of sight on the rear with 1A88 1158 Penzance-London Paddington. *8 August 2015*

As previously mentioned, Devonport GWR served what was a proud and independent borough and this was reflected in the importance given to the station which for a wayside one was of a substantial construction. This is the rather imposing view of the station exterior, with its own canopy covering almost the full length of the structure. One did not wait for one's car or taxi, or in a previous era horse and carriage, here in the rain. Close inspection of the signs by the red ticket collector's hut indicate the way to the booking office and waiting rooms. Another directs prospective passengers 'To Up and Down' trains, the GWR obviously confident its prospective travellers were aware of their direction of travel. On the wall there is one of the once familiar blue 'You may telephone from here' signs, once so common – and useful in the era before the mobile phone had even been conceived. This was also the station designated as the rail head for the Torpoint Ferry, which is just down the road, and it was through here that all manner of perishable and parcels traffic came to serve what was once a thriving and prosperous town in its own right, and one often recalled to me by my mother who was a Devonport girl. *22 September 1969*

There's not a lot to really add to the present-day scene. The station building was swept away in the autumn of 1969. Remarkably the telegraph pole to the left is common to both pictures with the arc of the road and the chimney of the building to the left of the Havelock Terrace overbridge also recognisable features. Not much protection from the elements these days if one has to wait outside the station for a lift or a taxi. *4 March 2015*

DEVONPORT ALBERT ROAD LOOKING EAST

This fine view looking east is taken from the steps of the former signal box. It shows how the station was built on the curve which takes the line from its east-west axis to a north-south one to run inland of the River Tamar until the latter could be bridged at Saltash, and how its eastern end in particular was hemmed in by being constructed partially in a cutting. Even so, it was an imposing station. The building on the 'Up', left hand side, was not insignificant with a large 'apex' canopy to protect east-bound prospective travellers from the elements. It is a further reminder of how much importance the GWR gave in serving the Borough of Devonport. In its day this was a busy station served, until the run down of the Saltash suburban services, by up to 30 trains a day in each direction. The station saw a sharp decline in the late 1960s and became unstaffed as from 19 May 1969. *22 September 1969*

Recent cutting back of foliage and use of my little portable step ladder by the line side fence almost recreates the angle from the former signal box steps. Sadly, the shot is rather depressing compared to the one above, but the curve of the line and platform – the 'Down' one shortened by a few yards, the colour light signal rear view, a new footbridge installed circa 2008, not too far removed from the position of its forebear and the Havelock Terrace overbridge – give us our bearings. 'Sprinter' 150 265 makes the station stop with 2P84 1145 Gunnislake-Plymouth. *4 March 2015*

The 125-yard Devonport Tunnel is built on a curve and is a shallow structure as it passes beneath Exmouth Road at its junction with Albert Road. It also has a unique feature that exists but can't be seen. Let me explain: the rear portion of each train in the two images would be passing over Ford Tunnel on the former Southern route from Devonport Junction to St Budeaux. Disused since 1964 and blocked, but it is still there. The crown of Ford Tunnel is only four feet from the rails in the Great Western Tunnel above. It is difficult to illustrate two tunnels with one passing beneath the other and I hope this description has clarified this very unusual occurrence.

A striking portrait of maroon liveried Class 52 D1016 'Western Gladiator' (again at Devonport) emerging from Devonport Tunnel with 7C56 St Blazey-Tavistock Junction goods. This nice clear view was taken to the rear of the former signal box and the advertising hoardings in Exmouth Road can be spotted above the tunnel portal. *23 September 1969*

The view today is a little further back from that above and is from the carpark fence. With the advertising hoardings long since gone and much greenery pruned, we get a view of the former Kimber's Garage with its far-left-facing south wall which is actually right above the southern entrance to Ford Tunnel. 43144 in 'Building a Greater West' livery heads out of the tunnel with 1A83 1000 Penzance-London Paddington with 43197 out of sight on the rear, just about on top of Ford Tunnel. *4 March 2015*

DOCKYARD HALT

This is a station whose name denotes the reason for its very existence. Opened on 1 June 1905, it was the last of the stopping places between Devonport and Saltash to be constructed, one year after the introduction of the steam rail motor service when the GWR rather belatedly realised the potential of the suburban traffic. North Gate and South Gate were once very familiar terms to workers employed in HM Dockyard. These are known today as St Levan and Albert Gates respectively and the station that remains open is convenient for both, being mainly served by the Plymouth-Gunnislake Branch trains and a handful of mainline local services. The suffix 'Halt' was dropped in May 1969 when the original GWR unusual style 'pagoda' shelters were removed.

A replacement was provided on the left hand, 'Down' platform so passengers waiting for a train to Plymouth just had to hope it didn't rain! In recent years the station has appeared in the time table as Dockyard Devonport.

A Christmas card scene (actually taken nearer to Easter than Christmas) from the Pasley Street overbridge looking west with the original GWR pagodas on show, and the chimneys in Goschen Yard visible to the left of Keyham Cutting in the far background. *March 1968*

The snow has melted, the GWR pagodas are long gone, the Goschen Yard chimneys are no more and there is a lot of greenery, but it is still a very recognisable scene as 66 030 passes through with 6C45 1252 Burngullow-Exeter Riverside Goods. *11 September 2007*

Although not apparent in the view off the Pasley Street overbridge, the main line crosses Keyham Viaduct and that will be discussed next. The rear half of the train, above, is still on the structure and before the tracks pass through Keyham or Goschen Cutting there was yet another station, Ford Halt, opened on 1 June 1904, to tap the growing suburban traffic on the introduction of the Plymouth-Saltash steam rail motor service. It was only 19 chains from Dockyard Halt and 25 chains from Keyham Station, such were the demands for the suburban service. It was roughly equidistant from the Southern Railway Ford Station that was at the other end of Station Road, surely one of the few Station Roads to actually have a station at each end! The thoroughfare still exists today but the stations do not. Ford Halt was closed on 6 November 1941 as the result of heavy enemy bombing in the area. Some remnants of the brick platforms remain but access to the precise spot is nigh on impossible. Let Dockyard Halt's pictures also tell the tale of its close neighbour. 'Britannia' Class pacific 70 013 'Oliver Cromwell' passes a deserted Dockyard Halt where the only change since 2007 has been further growth with 1Z45 1745 Par-Bristol Temple Meads. *5 August 2012*

I would have let the top picture complete the Dockyard and Ford Halt's story, but wind on two years and there is a further change to the scene here. Look to the far left of the Keyham or Goschen cutting where the chimneys appear in the first picture of the snow of 1969 for there is a new landmark on the horizon. It's the tall chimney of the newly constructed MW Environment Devonport Ltd Incinerator, our introduction to a controversial structure which will feature very much as we progress through Keyham and St Budeaux. 'Black 5' 45 407 drifts by with 1Z39 1745 Par-Bristol Temple Meads. *6 July 2014*

KEYHAM VIADUCT

Although much has been lost of the railway infrastructure in Plymouth, there is one feature unsung and often overlooked, which is worthy of attention in its own right. I recommend anyone to stand in St Levan Road and gaze up at its strong metal spans, and impressive piers of interwoven brickwork, built on the original Brunel masonry piers. This is Keyham Viaduct which carries the Cornish main line 88 feet above the St Levan Valley. Much like Stonehouse Pool, when the railway was built here in the 1850s the local scene was very different from that of today. The railway had to cross Keyham Lake in a rural setting, the waters then extending the length of what is now St Levan Road. The original wooden structure was replaced in 1899, around the same time as surrounding housing was being developed, and the 1899 steelwork was itself replaced in 1937 when extra brickwork was added to some of the piers to give the very fine viaduct that graces the scene today.

The view from the MOD playing fields as Class 52 D1037 'Western Empress' passes over Keyham Viaduct with 1V76 Liverpool-Penzance with St Levan Road to the right and behind Ford Viaduct, which we shall revisit in due course; this carried the Southern main line over the Valley. *20 March 1974*

The playing fields are now out of bounds so we move to the right a few yards to stand in St Levan Road to look upon this superb structure. 150 120 crosses the valley with 2G76 1540 Plymouth-Gunnislake. The main change is, of course, the removal of Ford Viaduct in 1986. In the distance, behind the piers, the yellow outline of the Plymouth Life Centre, opened in March 2012, is a new feature to the skyline. *19 April 2015*

The panorama of Keyham and its station from the Royal Navy Avenue overbridge looking north towards Saltash. The washing is out in the gardens of Admiralty Street to the right. The station, although by now unstaffed, still has the appearance of a typical GWR wayside stopping place, the goods shed still standing but not in railway use. Still operational are the two lines in the Yard, the 'Up' loop still able to take a passenger train with the 'Up' siding still available to serve the daily train that served the Dockyard, Bull Point and Ernesettle Siding. To the left is Johnston Terrace and a very familiar landmark, the Royal Naval Barracks' Clock. In the far background the Bull Point housing estate of the mid-1950s forms the skyline. It all looks neat and tidy as Class 47 D1637, later 47 483, passes by with the Sunday 1A48 1005 Penzance-London Paddington. I suspect there was probably some questionable language used when the 47 turned up instead of a Class 52 'Western' but what would I give now to see one of these pass by on a London train! *27 July 1969*

Other than the chance to study some trees close up, there is not much of a panorama now to be enjoyed from the Royal Navy Avenue overbridge. The curve of the line through the station can be marked out, some of the background houses can be glimpsed with a little of the Bull Point skyline visible, and the Royal Naval Barracks' Clock still keeps good time and is still visible to the left. Sadly, it's another location where trains can be more heard than seen. *4 March 2015*

KEYHAM, WHERE IT ALL BEGAN

A question I am frequently asked is "how and where did my love of railways start?" The answer is right here – Admiralty Street and the footbridge at Keyham Station. The first decade of my life was spent in Victory Street, with only Fleet Street in between home and the railway line. When I was in the pushchair my grandfather, William Mills, took me here to watch the trains go by and that, quite simply, is how it all started. My early memories are of 4037 'South Wales Borderers', one of the 'Star' Class rebuilt as a 'Castle' on an 'Up' Express, 5098 'Clifford Castle' rushing through alternately every other day with 1010 'County of Caernarvon' on the 'Up' 'Cornishman' as the Barracks' Clock showed the time as 1245. Then there were 6407, 6419, and 6421 busily going about their duties pulling and pushing the 'Saltash Motor' as my parents described what I thought was a fussy little train. So that is the simple story of where it all began.

The scene from the Admiralty Street end of the footbridge, and by this time I could afford a camera with colour film. Nothing had changed from my early childhood view of the railway. A Plymouth bound DMU arrives passing the signal box with the lines in the yard intact and the small grocery warehouse to the right. *August 1966*

By the time we see Class 25 D7575 in the yard on an engineering train, little had changed save for the removal, on 24 February 1966, of the loop into the goods shed. The small warehouse, which I think supplied Lyons Tea, was still open for business, note the Triumph Herald and the mini van. *22 March 1973*

The view from the footbridge today. There is not one from Admiralty Street, since the houses were built in 2001, and it is still a recognisable scene. Only the 'Up' loop remains in the Yard, and I suspect not for much longer. The signal box, closed in July 1973, and the warehouse are long gone. Just beyond the Saltash Road overbridge we get a glimpse of a new feature, the North Yard Incinerator. 150 265 heads away with 2G74 1054 Plymouth-Gunnislake. *4 March 2015*

KEYHAM STATION FOOTBRIDGE WITH DMUs

Three pictures featuring various types of Diesel Multiple Unit and the view looking towards Devonport, from the footbridge at Keyham Station. The platforms and Alexandra Park with the background houses remain constant.

Back to the summer of 1966, when England won the World Cup, and Bubble Car W55029 departs for Dockyard Halt with a Saltash-Plymouth service. Of particular interest in the background are the signals for the main line and to exit the 'Up' loop, these being the standard Western Region semaphores but with a colour-light distant for the Plymouth Panel acting as a lower arm distant, a very unusual arrangement. *July 1966*

The sun is still shining as the experimental unit 140 001 – the prototype for the dreaded 'Pacer' units – runs in with the 1811 Plymouth-Gunnislake, a journey I well remember as this was the train that took both myself and many friends and colleagues to Calstock for my stag night at the Boot Inn! The station buildings have been demolished and a 'bus stop' shelter has been provided for Plymouth-bound passengers, the signals have been removed (in July 1973 when the Plymouth Panel took control of the area) and there has been some development in Admiralty Street (on the site of the former Methodist Church), otherwise the scene is much the same. *8 May 1985*

Thirty years on the main changes are the 2000/2001 additional housing developments in Admiralty Street, removal of the 'Up' siding with new fencing, a very up-to-date waiting shelter, CCTV cameras, modern lighting and vegetation blocking the view of the Royal Navy Avenue overbridge. 'Sprinter' 150 247 departs with 2P91 1545 Gunnislake-Plymouth. *21 April 2015*

KEYHAM STATION

Keyham Station opened on 2 July 1900 to serve the growing population and the HMS *Drake* part of the Naval Base (first occupied in 1889), in association with the doubling of the line from the south, that was completed at the same time. It was built very much in the style of the GWR of the period. Both platforms had brick buildings containing a booking office, with apex-style canopies supplemented by a metal hut, the one on the 'Down' platform, Cornwall-bound, served as the Parcels and Left Luggage Office and in my day had been rebuilt in concrete. The 'Up' one, seen here to the right with a luggage barrow outside, served as an additional waiting room. This is the view looking north towards Saltash with Admiralty Street (on the right), the footbridge that crossed the yard and also the station lamp posts which bore oil lamps. I well remember the glow of these on a dark winter's night as they swayed in the wind. Keyham was then still a busy suburban station with workers especially going to and from the adjacent Naval Base, which itself provided a lot of traffic. *August 1966*

Much has changed over the years although the scene is still recognisable. To the right the housing developments of 2000/2001 have altered the view of Admiralty Street. The footbridge appears as two separate and rebuilt halves. Network Rail own the green section over the tracks while the City Council own the right hand side and the railway company claim they are only obliged to provide a safe route between the platforms, not a shortcut for the local population. Politics at its very best I do believe. The station was unstaffed from May 1969 with the buildings demolished in the mid-1970s. Those romantic oil lamps are but a memory in the era of electric time switch controlled lighting. 'Britannia' Class 70013 'Oliver Cromwell' hurries through with 1Z35 1745 Par-Bristol 'Royal Duchy', recalling memories of the 1950s when this Class, but not this particular specimen, worked through here on the Penzance expresses. *8 September 2013*

Behind the train in the top two pictures on page 58, we saw Keyham Station Signal Box. It was opened in 1900 as part of the works of doubling the track with a 33-lever frame, increased to 59 levers when a new frame was installed in 1937. 4911 Bowden Hall took a direct hit from a bomb outside the signal box in an air raid on 30 April 1941. The engine was damaged beyond repair. On 26 November 1960 Keyham became the west-bound fringe box for the Plymouth Panel and was closed on 2 July 1973 when the Plymouth Panel was extended, St Germans becoming the fringe box. It was also the only signal box I ever worked officially. Back in 1964 when I joined the railway all staff were encouraged to learn how the railway worked, and how other departments did their job. I took the rules course out of interest and passed my exams and actually learnt and signed for the frames at Keyham, Royal Albert and Saltash Signal Boxes. One spring morning in 1966 I was working in the booking office at Keyham when the duty signalman, Alfie Freeman, was taken ill and I was summonsed to take over until a relief signalman was able to come and take duty. So for a couple of hours I had full control of a section of the West of England main line.

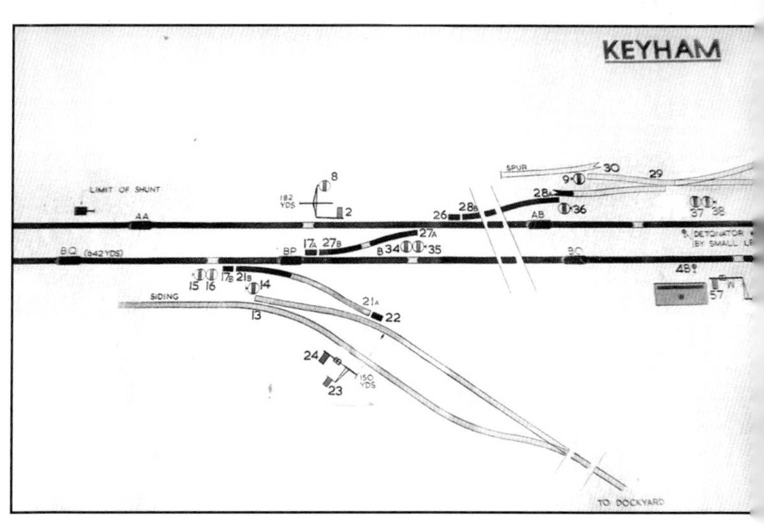

We can pay a visit on Christmas Eve with one of the regular signalmen here, Tommy Hunn. The block instruments and bells are on the shelf above the frame. Note the signalman's chair in the left hand corner.

An evocative view of the south end of the frame. *Both 24 December 1965*

Courtesy of Ron Andrews, who was a relief signalman for the district, a part of the signal box diagram showing the junction with the Dockyard Line that we are about to visit. *Undated 1973*

KEYHAM, THE DOCKYARD JUNCTION

This is another view that has matured over the years: looking north past the junction with the line into Dockyard on the left, across Weston Mill Viaduct towards St Budeaux, with the Bull Point Estate high on the hill behind.

Class 52 D1064 'Western Regent' passes the Dockyard Line Junction with a well-loaded nine coach 1Z03 0850 Penzance-Paignton, August Bank Holiday Monday Excursion. Yes, the railway really did run trains like that, with the rear of the train just coming off Weston Mill Viaduct. This four-span steel girder construction with three masonry approach arches on either end was completed in 1903 replacing the rather flimsy looking timber viaduct, of 1859, that was at a lower level and on a different alignment to the right. There was much construction and track alteration work here at this time along with the elimination of the 1-in- 60 gradients at both ends. The original alignment of the track at the lower level is clearly visible, becoming incorporated to the very useful (but now closed) footpath that was attached to the viaduct. On the left is the former swimming pool in HMS *Drake*, behind, a clear view of Camels Head Creek. *27 August 1973*

We move on to the new century where perhaps one change that catches the eye is the very bright blue paint of the reinforced fence for the footpath. Other changes are that the swimming pool has been spruced up, the inevitable growth and the major change is Camels Head Creek, reclaimed in 1974/75 to provide further expansion for the Naval Base, of which more later. Only a fortnight before the end of daily cross country locomotive-hauled trains, 47 851, repainted into the original 1960s two tone green livery, passes by with 1M56 0846 Penzance-Manchester Piccadilly. *2 August 2002*

A fairly short time span between this and the lower image of the previous page, but the scene has further evolved with the footpath to the right, which crossed the viaduct, now closed. Neither Network Rail or the City Council would pay for the work to maintain it despite its popularity, and yet it did cut off a lot of ground for pedestrians. It is now a long walk to St Budeaux around Camels Head, the alternatives being to catch a train or bus. The principal change in the scene is in the Naval Base with the new transport hub, constructed to handle all the big lorries that now carry all the freight traffic in and out, material that previously mostly came and went by train. 66 205 brings 6S55 Burngullow-Irvine clay slurry past the Dockyard Junction, a train that ran for the last time on 29 January 2008. *November 2007*

So to the present day, with Plymouth's new landmark, the recently constructed and at the time still-being-commissioned incinerator, a controversial structure built in North Yard to take Plymouth's and much else of South Devon's refuse to provide energy for the Naval Base. I will not get involved with the politics or controversy, but one has to wonder if it is the wrong thing in the wrong place. It certainly now dominates this scene blocking a part of the view of and from the Bull Point Estate. The other main changes are in the amount of the foliage, especially to the right and in front of the former swimming pool, (closed and subsequently demolished, unfortunately unwanted water was coming in where it shouldn't, causing a problem with dampness) and Weston Mill Viaduct has changed colour. Over the years we have witnessed this scene evolve but it is still very recognisable. 43005 (front), 43127 (rear) trundle past with 1A81 0844 Penzance-London Paddington. *4 March 2015*

THE DOCKYARD BRANCH

The connection from the Cornwall Railway main line into the Dockyard was unusual in that it was always Government owned and, as it was built over private land and did not convey any public traffic, it did not require an Act of Parliament. It opened in June 1867 as a broad-gauge line. Nine years later the LSWR arrived at Devonport.

A standard-gauge rail was added to the Cornwall main line from Devonport Junction to a point ten chains beyond the Dockyard line junction (and, of course, to the branch as well) to allow LSWR access; this was at the behest of the Admiralty, who sought a through-transit for their traffic without the inconvenience of transhipment between gauges.

It should also be noted that the original junction was at a different elevation and was greatly altered and repositioned in the already mentioned work of building the new Weston Mill Viaduct.

Take a look at the part of the Keyham Station Signal Box diagram reproduced on Page 61 and this is a pictorial view to go with it. The signal in the 'off' position is K24. Just behind it is the green Dockyard Signal Box that issued the single token for the branch. Beyond is the main line and in the far distance the embankment that once carried the Southern Main Line through Weston Mill. Here we have the extremely rare sight of a passenger train on the line, a three car DMU forms the 1220 Admiralty Platform-Portsmouth Naval Special, the very last passenger train to run from Admiralty Platform, which I will mention when I turn round and look the other way from this overbridge, just outside HMS *Drake*. *10 December 1971*

Sadly the goods traffic to and from the Naval Base was lost to rail over the years and the 1982 Falklands War can be said to be the final era of regular freight traffic to and from the Dockyard. It finally ceased in 1984 and the line has been infrequently used since. The decline is evident in this changing scene which resembles more that of a rusty, overgrown and forgotten railway. An unidentified Class 33 slowly makes its way onto the branch. Of particular note in the background, the Southern Line Embankment has vanished. *August 1984*

Since the cessation of regular freight traffic to and from the Dockyard in 1984, the branch sees little activity these days and its only use now, other than any rolling stock contracts that may arise, is for the transit of nuclear flasks to and from Sellafield in Cumbria. So infrequent is this that it may only happen once or twice in a year. This is, believe it or not, the only freight traffic to be conveyed by rail out of the whole City of Plymouth. Perhaps in these days of climate change and the carbon footprint, here is one for the Green lobby to take up.

The obvious change since the pictures on the previous page are the removal, in Spring 1992, of the rails on the left, leading to the head shunt, leaving just a single track here, and the untidy and overgrown forgotten branch line scene somewhat tidied up with the vegetation cut back, a welcome occurrence. There is no evidence in the far background by now of the former Southern route through Weston Mill. Here we have a rare appearance of the nuclear flask train coming off the main line in to the Dockyard. 47 293 propels the train 6X91 1650 (previous day) Sellafield-Keyham Dockyard on to the branch for the short journey to the Exchange Sidings. *16 August 1995*

The present-day scene – a train on the Dockyard Branch is sadly a rare sight, but observe that from the stop sign for the main line, which acts as the boundary with Network Rail, the MOD-owned track is well maintained and free of weeds and growth. The small MOD Signal Box has disappeared, following a vandal attack, I do not have a date for this. There has been a substantial investment in lighting for the line here given the number of lampposts that have sprouted. How often they are needed is another matter. *30 May 2015*

ADMIRALTY PLATFORM

Turning around the other way on the overbridge by the Dockyard Line Junction we see Admiralty Platform which, like the former Ocean Terminals at Millbay and Stonehouse Pool, never appeared in public time tables. Opened in October 1886, coinciding with the establishment of HMS *Drake*, its main use was for Forces' Specials that ran as and when required. Operation of those bound for the GWR Line heading east involved a reversal at the main line junction requiring a locomotive at either end, a time consuming and cumbersome arrangement, that goes some way to explaining why the 'Up' platform loop at Keyham was fitted for passenger working, as Naval specials also started there. Operation of trains heading for the Southern Main Line became much simpler when the World War II connection was installed at St Budeaux, a feature we shall discuss in due course. The original stone construction was enhanced by a timber extension at the main line end at the advent of World War I. This was removed in the mid-1970s, but the original stone platform remains 'in situ'.

This is the only known photograph of a passenger train at Admiralty Platform – the 1220 Naval Special to Portsmouth for Christmas leave in 1971. As far as I am aware, this was also the last passenger train to start out at the station, although it was used for an incoming special on 30 March 1985 and the following year for a ceremony involving 50 032 'Courageous' receiving a crest from its namesake. *10 December 1971*

The view looks very similar today with the overbridge forming the entrance to HMS *Drake* and the Barracks' Clock our unchanged landmarks. Sadly the rails have a rusty look as few trains pass this way at present. The extreme east end, the stone part of the platform, can just be seen under the bridge leading to HMS *Drake* by the Barracks' Clock. Careful observation will note the platform edge is still painted white despite not being used for many years. Look to the right and for a change, the growth is less than the original scene revealing the concrete wall built at some time in the intervening years. *26 April 2015*

The Devonport Dockyard Railway was notable in a number of ways. Firstly, at just two miles in length, it was one of the smallest State-owned railways in the world. It was always a part of the Admiralty/MOD and ran independently of the national system. Secondly, it had more classes of passenger accommodation than route miles of track. Passenger comfort ranged from blue upholstery down to bare wood in five classes designated as follows: 'Principal Dockyard Officers', 'Superior and Commissioned Officers', 'Subordinate Officers', 'Chargemen, Recorders and Petty Officers', 'Workmen and Ratings'. Thirdly, being purely an internal service, it was free to use and therefore had no need of a ticketing system. The line connected North and South Yards, separated by the road to the Torpoint Ferry, by means of a three-quarter-mile tunnel opened for goods in 1857. The passenger service, which ran half-hourly during the day, was introduced in 1900 and withdrawn on 13 May 1965 on completion of a road bridge over the Torpoint Ferry road.

By the early 1960s services were mostly diesel worked, however an immaculate No 17 was turned out for a PRC visit, and is seen at the North Yard terminus ready to leave for South Yard, the typical train in correct formation with the lowest class accommodation at the rear of a southbound service. *27 March 1963*

Much has changed within this part of the Naval Base; the surviving freight-only railway was realigned here in 2000. There are a couple of common links between the two images, one is the wall carrying the pipe line, this is visible just to the right of No 17, and in the background, to the left, the red-brick building used as a store survives intact. *10 July 2015*

No 17 has arrived at the North Yard terminus with a train from South Yard, thus the view is looking south. The wooden rolling stock was constructed in the Dockyard, and each train also conveyed an open flat-bed, four-wheel freight wagon for the conveyance of 'luggage' such as tool boxes, lunch boxes, light goods and bicycles. This was always positioned next to the workmen's carriages. Higher rank accommodation always occupied the two coaches at the south end of the train. This is a classic industrial dockland railway scene with its cranes and buildings. *27 March 1963*

Much has changed as this part of North Yard was substantially rebuilt and the course of the surviving railway altered in 2000. The former route to South Yard has been completely removed, the re-routed railway to the Exchange Sidings is out of camera range behind the buildings to the left, the modern construction overtaking those of the older order. To the right, the flank of the large crane, a city landmark, provides the necessary link between the two images. My thanks to Paul Burkhalter and Messrs Babcock, and their staff, for their help in arranging this visit to update some very rare pictures, and for permission to publish. *10 July 2015*

Not the best quality picture, but a very rare one of a passenger train just about to enter the Burma Narrows on the approach to the former Albert Gate. Relaying information provided by former Dockyard employees, the buildings behind the train are the coppersmith's pipe shop. To the left are 81 shop Ship-Wrights and 79 shop Turning- lathes. The tracks in the foreground lead out from the former locomotive sheds. It's a good opportunity to study the four-wheel wooden rolling stock. Next to the engine is vehicle number 34, for the higher class of travellers, followed by number 26 with its more limited window view for the lesser mortals. The basic design is very simple. The inscription 'SNSO' indicates the stock was under the control of the Senior Naval Stores Officer. *2 November 1964*

Through the good efforts of Paul Burkhalter and Messrs Babcock I was able to find the precise spot, easily identified by the bungalow-type building behind the diesel engine in the top picture and the building still extant to the left. The coppersmith's pipe shop has long since gone revealing the dockyard wall, 79 and 81 shops have made way for a carpark, and there is little evidence that trains once passed through here, unless one ventures into the carpark for a closer look. *10 July 2015*

Into the carpark here, at the entrance to Burma Narrows, there is still 'in situ' a small section of one of the curves seen in the top picture, leading in the direction of South Yard. Otherwise precious little remains of this part of the system. *10 July 2015*

THE DEVONPORT DOCKYARD RAILWAY

One from the family album, the group picture taken by Ivor Hocking of the PRC visit in March 1963. The MOD would only allow one camera with colour film in the party, so we all paid for the film and Ivor took every picture a number of times so that those who wished had an original slide – one way around the photographic restrictions! Standing in front of No 17 from left to right the people are: Locomotive Driver, Chris Soper (Chairman of the PRC), Mr Robbins (I think), Keith Holt, Alan Weary, the author (aged 16), Ken Holdaway (President of the PRC at the time), Bernard Murton (Hon Secretary of the PRC from its founding in 1948 to 1963), RC Sambourne (PRC Treasurer and a name much recalled in the annals of Plymouth City Transport), Harry Liddle (founder member of the PRC and Dockyard Locomotive Inspector). *27 March 1963*

To many a frustrated railway passenger the term 'rail replacement bus service' conjours up thoughts of woe, inconvenience and over-running engineering work. Or one may think of a town or village given a replacement bus service for that long-since closed station or branch line, which has then gone the same way as the train it replaced. Here is a rail replacement with a difference, the free bus service which runs through the Dockyard from Camel's Head Gate to Granby Gate, seen here running along the Burma Narrows on the course of the former passenger railway. One assumes the Admiral and the Labourer share the same space as the bus does not have five classes of accommodation. Equality for all in the modern age.

The passenger service on the Dockyard Railway did not serve actual stations as such and thus did not have platforms, it called at a number of recognised stopping places one of which was Albert Gate, and I was quite amazed to find, on my recent visit, a bus stop provided at what was the train stopping point where the train emerged from the Burma Narrows. The rails may well have gone, with the passenger train a distant memory, but one can still join the free rail replacement bus service at what was a recognised place to join the train. Amazing. *10 July 2015*

After our visit into the Dockyard, our journey resumes at the northern end of Weston Mill Viaduct. There were major engineering works here in 1903, when the new viaduct was constructed. The original alignment was to the right where the footpath continues towards St Budeaux, originally rising by a 1-in-60 gradient to the left to join the route into Cornwall. Both pictures are taken from the footpath bolted on to the viaduct and are looking towards Saltash.

Class 43 'Warship' D842 'Royal Oak' passing with 1M99 1305 Penzance-Liverpool Lime Street. To the left, the Bull Point Estate on the hill, to the right Wolseley Road and the masonry arch which took the SR route on its way through Weston Mill towards Devonport Junction, a feature we shall take a closer look at in due course. *April 1966*

This is taken only seven years later and there is one major change - the former arch over Wolseley Road which carried the SR main line has been demolished. An unidentified single car DMU heads for Plymouth with the 1330 Liskeard-Plymouth. Both trains are passing the St Budeaux Ferry Road 'Up' starting signal with lower arm distant for Keyham. Access to this location now is impossible, and as will be gained from other updated pictures of this area to follow in the next few pages, the view if one could see it through the growth would be very different. *22 June 1973*

WESTON MILL VIADUCT FROM BULL POINT

The present day Weston Mill Viaduct was built on a new alignment with raised track levels just to the west of the rather flimsy looking original Brunel timber viaduct of 1859. Its design was unique to the former Cornwall Railway main line, comprising four sets of steel bowstring girders, resting on three round caisson piers in mid span with three masonry arch approaches at either end. Brought in to use in 1903, the structure carries the railway over Camel's Head Creek, a tidal inlet of the River Tamar. Like Keyham Viaduct it is somewhat overshadowed by the Royal Albert Bridge although it is a fine piece of engineering in own right.

The first of four views taken from Poole Park Road showing how the viaduct and the railway remain constant, but the creek certainly does not. Class 43 'Warship' D857 'Undaunted' heads west with 1C60 1430 London Paddington-Penzance. High tide on a summer evening gives an almost exotic look to the scene Do not be fooled, at low tide it presented an ugly sea of mud with an aroma all of its own. *8 June 1968*

In the early 1970s Camel's Head Creek was infilled as part of the extension of North Yard. Work is well under way in transforming the scene as the now preserved Class 52 D1015 'Western Champion' heads for Cornwall with 1V76 0920 Liverpool Lime Street-Penzance. *17 May 1974*

WESTON MILL VIADUCT FROM BULL POINT

Camel's Head Creek is no more, in this transformed scene, as an unidentified Class 47 heads along with the 0825 Glasgow Central-Penzance. The background scene of Wombwell Crescent and the Keyham streets look much the same, as does North Down Park to the top left. The former creek has been completely infilled and the site now forms one of the main entrances to the extended Naval Base. The viaduct looks very smart after a new coat of paint. *14 July 1990*

The viaduct and the extended Naval Base are still there, it is just that due to rampant growth they are barely visible, although close examination to the right reveals the bowstring girders of the viaduct are now painted blue. Even the vantage point has changed with the provision of a little park. Beyond the growth the background line of houses acts as a good link to the images of the past. *21 April 2015*

ST BUDEAUX JUNCTION FROM ABOVE

The view from Cardinal Avenue looking south west towards the Gunnislake line junction with to the right Blackie Woods and the flats adjacent to Bull Point, behind the train further infilling reclamation of Camels Head Creek is underway and beyond we see a panorama of the North Yard of the Naval Base with the River Tamar, Torpoint and the hills of South East Cornwall stretching away in to the distance. In the foreground we see the top of the former SR cutting leading towards Weston Mill next to a traffic free Wolseley Road. In this splendid image captured by my good friend Barry Jones from Laira, 50 004 "St Vincent" is seen heading towards Plymouth with what is more than likely the London bound "Cornish Riviera" immediately before this service was turned over to HST operation. *28 March 1979*

The present day view is recognisable to that of 1979; the Sprinter taking the Gunnislake Branch is in exactly the same place where we see 50 004 above. Hidden by growth and housing are the former SR cutting and Wolseley Road, but is on the other side of the tracks we see how the landscape has been transformed by the construction of the Incinerator within the North Yard boundary of the Naval Base, the view looking towards the Dockyard and Torpoint is still visible, perhaps the most noticeable change here being the removal of the towering Dockyard crane, this in itself once another local landmark. With all the development, an unwanted and unloved (certainly by the locals) new landmark, trains pass by here now in a very different setting to that of the past. 150 249 with 2G74 1054 Plymouth-Gunnislake heads over the cross over from the "Down" to the "Up" main line to make its way on to the branch. On the next couple of pages we will have a ground level look the tracks and signals here in the era of mechanical signalling. *21 April 2015*

St Budeaux became a full-time junction between two railway lines on the closure of the SR route from Victoria Road to Devonport Junction from 7 September 1964. The SR main line became the Gunnislake Branch, from 6 May 1968, upon the closure of the route beyond Bere Alston. This was singled from 7 September 1970 causing an alteration to the physical junction of a Gunnislake-bound train to the modified single line.

A driver's-eye-view from the cab where we saw D857 and 150 249 on the previous page. In a way this defines the setting of the railway at St Budeaux where the Southern, on its entrance to Plymouth, brushed alongside its rival the GWR, wartime need connecting the two. The view is looking towards Saltash with the junction signal a splendid GWR wooden post bracket specimen, the left-hand arm with lower arm fixed distant for Royal Albert Bridge Signal Box, and the right arm, which has been pulled off, is for the Gunnislake Branch. Beyond the GWR signal box we see the former SR goods shed in what was Victoria Road goods yard, a view now obscured by the Lidl store. The Bull Point Branch diverges to the left between the parked cars. *May 1967*

Not long after the above picture was taken, the splendid GWR wooden post bracket signal was replaced by the standard Western Region steel tubular version with metal arms. The GWR had introduced use of tubular steel in place of wood for bracket signals in 1942. To accommodate the new arrangements for accessing the single line to Gunnislake by a single-lead junction, the junction bracket signal was moved approximately 200 yards further towards Keyham on 23 August 1970. The re-sited position of the signal is very noticeable when studying the two pictures. Two other changes in those six years are the demolition of the former SR goods shed, and the tree growth to the left. Today a colour-light signal, worked from Plymouth, controls the junction and, like the SR goods shed, both the signal box and the mechanical signals are just a memory. *22 June 1973*

ST BUDEAUX FERRY ROAD SIGNAL BOX

The signal box here opened on 2 June 1916 with a 17-lever frame to coincide with the completion of the Bull Point Branch. A 36-lever frame was installed in March 1941 when the wartime connection with the SR line was established. Formerly known as St Budeaux East Signal Box, the name was altered to St Budeaux Ferry Road on the closure of St Budeaux West Signal Box as of 22 June 1952. It was closed on 2 July 1973 when the Plymouth Panel was extended to cover the area.

The wooden structure seen here is in its last weeks of operating life. Notice adjacent to the signal box steps the 250 milepost from Paddington via Bristol TM – Weston-Super-Mare avoiding line and Millbay. Despite the annihilation of the route in and out of Millbay, to this day all milepost readings west of Cornwall Loop Junction allow for the Millbay reversal.

A view of the 36 lever frame. A brief layman's guide to the lever colours: yellow = distant signal, red = running signals, black = points, blue = facing point locks, chevron = detonator lever. The block instruments are seen on the block shelf, note also the plungers which had to be pressed to release certain signals. Looking out beyond the signal box window the Cornish main line can be seen to the left, the Gunnislake branch going off to the right. *22 June 1973*

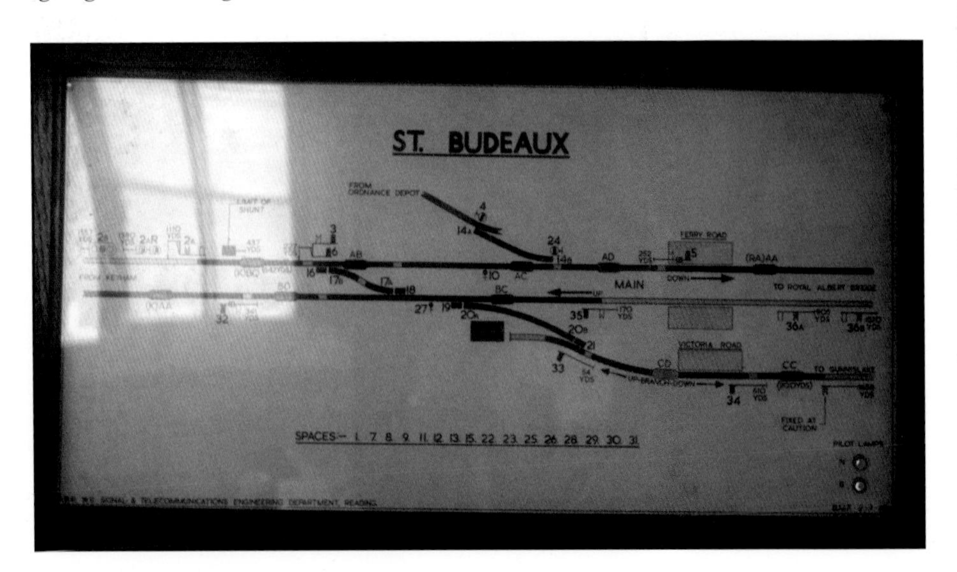

The signal box diagram in its final form after the creation of the single line Gunnislake Branch. The red light showing up in Victoria Road Station is a track circuit showing the branch as occupied. *22 June 1973*

Such was the volume of rail traffic to and from the local MOD bases that they were served by their own train that ran daily, Monday to Friday. Known locally as 'The Transfer', this ran from Tavistock Junction (later from Exeter Riverside) to Keyham. Arrival was around 0820 to split and shunt, and at 0930 (approximately) to go into the Dockyard with inward traffic. Returning to Keyham mid-morning, the Transfer would then take trips out to Ernesettle and/or Bull Point, before returning to Keyham, stabling, lunch for the crew, and then back into the Dockyard to collect originating traffic – and this was often substantial – before heading back to Keyham at about 1700. One of my jobs as a junior clerk at Keyham was to invoice goods traffic out of the Dockyard and telephone the Telegraph Office in Plymouth to advise such traffic forward. One regular flow was to Pridham's Yard at Gosport consigned under 'Green Arrow' conditions. The latter was a premium freight system inherited from the London & North Eastern Railway on Nationalisation in 1948 and adopted by British Railways. By 1982 the train had reduced in load sufficiently to be handled by a Class 08 diesel shunter and it finished altogether in 1984. Here are couple of very rare pictures of 'The Transfer' taken from St Budeaux Ferry Road Signal Box.

A superb study, above, of D6333 on the 'Down' main line after reversal from the Bull Point Branch, the line to the left. To the right is the Gunnislake Branch.

D6333, below, on the Bull Point Branch marking our introduction to this rarely photographed line, propelling its train onto the main line. *Both taken 13 September 1971*

One of the lesser-known and certainly rarely photographed branch lines in the City was the short – half a mile approximately – Bull Point Branch. It was one of the last lines to be constructed in the City. Thereafter – I seem to recall – there was only the adjacent connection between the Great Western and Southern Railways at St Budeaux in 1941, and the re-construction of the GWR Tavistock Branch by the Plym Valley Railway from the new station at Marsh Mills to Plym Bridge, finally completed in December 2012.

The area around St Budeaux Square was developed into a residential area in the early 1890s, merging with the Borough of Devonport in 1898. This in turn merged (unwillingly) with Plymouth in 1914 as the MOD wished to deal with one rather than three local authorities, due to the anticipated demands of the imminent war, and it was the latter that occasioned the construction of the short Bull Point Branch.

The waterside at Bull Point had been used as an out of the way location for gunpowder work in the Napoleonic Wars. In the mid Ninteenth Century the work here was enlarged by the relocation of magazines from Keyham Point to allow for construction of the Keyham Steam Yard. By 1915 Bull Point had become a major munitions plant. Despatch of its wares by sea was not a problem, those going inland had to be taken by horse and cart to the nearest railway station – St Budeaux Victoria Road. The increased wartime traffic led to the construction of the short branch from the GWR at St Budeaux to Bull Point which opened on 2 June 1916. Regular traffic ceased in 1984, and in 1990 the line was dismantled in a rather unique manner. The MOD donated all the track and fittings to the Plym Valley Railway. Their recovery and removal to Marsh Mills was quite a challenge, a story best left for the PVR annals.

The line was always freight only and as far as I know the only passenger train to traverse it was 'The Mayflower' Rail Tour formed of a five car DMU (for the record, this was formed by vehicles P479 51328+59509+51313 with P480 51327+51312), 1Z30 1115 from Newton Abbot having connected with a special 1Z30 locomotive-hauled 0705 from Paddington. The destination blind is rather ambitious showing 'Dulverton' where one would have seen such stock in the latter years of the Taunton-Barnstaple Branch, closed in October 1966. The trains that terminated at Dulverton were those off the Exe Valley Branch from Exeter St Davids via Tiverton, a line steam worked to its penultimate day in October 1963, when Class 22 diesels took over the workings to handle the crowds. The odd DMU did reach Tiverton, so yes we can romanticise a little on what one of these would have looked like in the leafier parts of the Exe Valley, even if we are in a rural part of Plymouth! *12 October 1980*

If one were travelling towards Cornwall on a mainline train and sat to the left, just after leaving Weston Mill Viaduct one could have caught sight of what appeared to be just another branch line curving away in to the woods. I suspect few people realised that those woods, with security reasons in mind, shielded the view of the terminus of what was in effect a long siding. The Bull Point Branch was worked under the control of the signalman at St Budeaux Ferry Road Signal Box with no single line token necessary. In my time as a relief clerk at Keyham I did once hitch a ride on the Transfer Goods over the line, but I was told to stay out of sight in the guard's van and dared not take out my camera as at the time photographers within sight of Bull Point were about as welcome there as motorists are now in a Plymouth bus lane.

A picture which also updates the view of St Budeaux Ferry Road Signal Box and the 250 milepost. If one looks beyond the gate the milepost can be seen, along with the relay room for the Plymouth Panel which replaced the mechanical signal box here in July 1973. I did a walk over the line in April1990 to record it in detail for posterity before the PVR moved in to claim the track. This is the curve away from the main line with the protecting gate for the branch; sadly, by now, we see a rundown scene in contrast to that of a decade earlier when the DMU came to call. *3 April 1990*

I undertook a similar walk a quarter of a century later to the month to record the changing scene. This is that same curve today from an identical viewpoint, only the bend of the former line, now a footpath, provides any link between the two images. High security fencing to protect the now out of sight main line and substantial growth have overtaken the view. *19 April 2015*

THE BULL POINT BRANCH

From the view looking towards the main line at the branch junction, we simply turn around at the same spot and look the other way.

The curve away from the main line took the branch through Blackie Woods. According to local legend, the woods are so named because of the dark soil and children who played here would get black with dirt, not that children anywhere in any era needed much excuse to come home with such evidence of childhood play! Going back to the railway, this is as about a rural country branch line scene as one would have found at countless locations all over the country. There is very little to suggest this charming railway byway scene is on a line built in a city environment, very close to housing development and bordering a major Naval Base. *4 April 1990*

For many years the course of the original railway here was heavily overgrown and it was a challenge to locate the former track bed. As part of the planning conditions for the adjacent Incinerator, opened in 2015 by MVV, one of the sops to appease the local population was the provision of a nature reserve in Blackie Woods. The former railway line was cleared and some excellent woodland management was undertaken to provide what is now a very useful facility. Whether the locals preferred having an Incinerator or an overgrown woodland is another matter. The curve of the former branch is well defined among the spring flowers, and maybe that alignment does just tell one that this was once a railway line. *19 April 2015*

Once around the short curve away from the main line, the branch gained the appearance of being double track. This was actually a run round loop, necessary as the actual terminus of the line, just out of sight around the corner by the background flats, consisted of three parallel sidings without any connecting points, so traffic had to be pulled in and propelled out or vice versa depending on the daily requirements. Any necessary shunting was carried out here. An interesting feature is the loading gauge, once a common sight in many a goods yard, station yard or branch line terminus. Quite simply any vehicle and/or load that was to travel anywhere on the railway network had to be able to pass beneath the suspended arch over the track without hitting or touching it, as it represented the maximum height of any tunnel, overbridge, station canopy, goods shed or any other feature that covered the track. If the train or any part of it could not pass under the loading gauge, it would not be allowed to travel until the correct measurements were met. The rule still applies today but with modern wagons, fixed-formation and container trains, the visible requirement for an old-style loading gauge has declined. The computer will tell the signalman if there is anything amiss. *3 April 1990*

The flats above the far end of the former loop remain to pinpoint the location. The track and the loading gauge are now at Marsh Mills and the newly constructed cycle path gives no indication that there were once twin railway tracks here. *19 April 2015*

The other end of the loop and the view looking back towards the main line with two of the sidings that ran into the terminus, that lay just behind the photographer. Despite its lowly one-(short)-train-a-day status by this time, the general view is one of a neat and tidy railway even though some of the rails show signs of rust. The DMU Rail Tour was only authorised to travel as far as the loop, so did not quite reach the stop blocks, nevertheless it made for an attractive and rather rare branch-line scene. The houses, top left, in Poole Park Road and, to the right, in Wolseley Road with those in Weston Mill, on the hill behind, make useful landmarks to mark the spot. *12 October 1980*

Other than the footpath following the curve of the line on what was the right hand track, there is nothing to link the two images. All traces of the railway have been swept away and the left hand side of the loop has become a wildflower meadow. Otherwise growth has overtaken the scene, blocking any view of the houses mentioned above. Hidden by the vegetation to the right is the new landmark – the Incinerator. One wonders how useful a rail link would be to bring in its waste and take away the ash it produces. It would not be difficult to construct. *19 April 2015*

This is the view looking from the west end of the loop, towards the end of the line. The lines passed through the security gate to enter the Bull Point Shed. This was by now out of use, with notices advising of dogs on patrol. As one can see MOD premises lay beyond the fence. Being a sensitive area, I dared go no further and beat a hasty retreat! The North Yard Dockyard crane is a good landmark. Railway-wise a rundown scene, but a very rare picture of one of the more obscure railway termini in the City. *3 April 1990*

The same vantage point but, like the rest of the former Bull Point Branch, it is a totally different scene today. This is where the footpath now leaves the former railway line, taking a right hand turn towards the access point in Talbot Gardens. The building to the left, part of the Incinerator, blocks the view of the Dockyard crane, and where the Bull Point railway terminal shed stood is best described as a large muddy patch. There are more recent signs on the security fence advising that dogs patrol the area. This advice is just about the only common link between the two pictures. *19 April 2015*

The station opened as St Budeaux Halt on 1 June 1904, the name changing to St Budeaux Platform in 1906 when the platforms were extended and further buildings provided. It became St Budeaux Ferry Road on 26 September 1949 to further distinguish between it and the adjacent Southern Railway Station. Running through is D1044 'Western Duchess' with 1A15 1030 Newquay-London Paddington and on each platform there is still a wooden waiting shed. The former 'pagodas' were demolished after the station was unstaffed in May 1969. There are two items of particular interest. The first is the Shell Garage behind the engine in Wolseley Road, this being crammed in a narrow space between the corresponding bridge to the adjacent Southern line. I recall that in the 1950s this garage was owned by a Jack Williams whose sisters ran the greengrocery shop in Victory Street, Keyham just doors from where I was first brought up. The second item to point out is the banner-repeating signal on the Cornwall-bound platform. This is purely a repeater for the actual signal just beyond the road bridge, giving train drivers advance warning of its indication. *16 June 1973*

The view today is instantly recognisable as a rare visitor in the form of A4 Pacific 60009 'Union of South Africa' speeds through with 1Z39 1745 Par-Bristol. The little modern-day waiting shelter on the 'Up' platform is obscured by the train. Passengers heading west have to hope it does not rain. Jack Williams' Garage is long gone, but a remarkable survivor is the banner-repeater signal, the original bracket still being used for the modern-day version controlled from the Plymouth Panel. The station remains open for a handful of local mainline services. *8 June 2013*

ST BUDEAUX WEST

Class 52 D1022 'Western Sentinel' passes by with 1E22 1005 Newquay-Newcastle. The line was doubled from St Budeaux to Royal Albert Bridge on 27 February 1902, the new formation being the 'Up', Plymouth-bound line which involved construction of a second and identical 'bow string' bridge at a slightly higher level over the Southern main line. On 28 June 1908 capacity was further enhanced by the installation of a 'Down' loop on the original single track formation of the main line from the west side of the 'bow string' bridge to Royal Albert. The east end of this was controlled from St Budeaux West Signal Box that opened at the same time. Advances in railway technology meant that the whole loop could be controlled from Royal Albert by motor points, this taking effect from 22 June 1952. The double-arm bracket signal, the banner repeater that we saw on the platform of Ferry Road Station, has the right hand arm pulled off for a 'Down' train to take the main line to Royal Albert, while the left hand arm gave access to the loop. *16 June 1973*

The present-day scene has a recognisable but untidy look. The line between St Budeaux Ferry Road and Royal Albert was singled upon the Plymouth Panel Signal Box taking control of the area on 2 July 1973 when the 'Down' loop was also taken out of use. The former 'Up' line of 1902 construction remains as the single line of route. The 'bow string' bridge on the Cornwall-bound line was subsequently demolished. A small engineer's yard has been established beside the remaining single line which meant that the updated picture was taken slightly to the left of the original where we see 150 202 + 153 373 pass by with 2E66 1205 Penzance-Exeter St Davids. *19 April 2015*

St Budeaux West Signal Box lay between the St Budeaux Ferry Road and Royal Albert Signal Boxes, and was very close to its neighbours on either side, situated 39 chains from St Budeaux East Signal Box and only 25 chains from Royal Albert, which was literally just around the corner. Its main purpose, as well as providing a further block section, was control of the east end of the 'Down' loop towards Royal Albert. The original structure, with a 21-lever frame, opened in 1908, and was bombed on the night of 28/29 April 1941, receiving a direct hit from a high-explosive bomb during an intensive air raid. It was replaced by a new structure, equipped with an identical lever frame and opened on 5 November 1941. But it would last for just over a decade, closing on 22 June 1952 when Royal Albert took over its duties. The disused signal box stood for over 20 years. I thank Ron Andrews for this splendid view of it with the houses of Pemros Road behind. *Undated circa 1972*

Below is a perfect example of "what man neglects, nature will reclaim". 47 439 passes St Budeaux West with the 1212 Penzance-London Paddington mail and vans, trains that were very colourful and are much missed since their demise in January 2004. It is hard to believe that where once there were three lines of rail there is now but one. The former 'Up' main line now serves as the single line; to the left the sites of the former 'Down' line and 'Down' loop have been completely overtaken by low level growth and brambles. Look behind the train for the common link between the two pictures – the houses of Pemros Road and the Devon-side tower of the Tamar Suspension Bridge. Lineside access here now would almost need an Act of Parliament. If one could update the picture, the foreground would be blocked with a combination of bushes and trees severely restricting the view. *19 September 1991*

ROYAL ALBERT DOWN LOOP

One of the more camera-shy Class 52s D1060 'Western Dominion' in charge of 1V76 0915 Liverpool Lime Street-Penzance is about to pass under Normandy Way. The view is looking towards St Budeaux showing the double track main line and the northern exit of the loop from St Budeaux West, then controlled from Royal Albert Bridge Signal Box. The loop – where many a freight train spent considerable time waiting for a path to cross the Royal Albert Bridge – looks rather rusty, but it was still operational. This was the original course of the single line, opened by the Cornwall Railway in May 1859. Things were about to change. *22 June 1973*

The main line was singled from St Budeaux Ferry Road to Royal Albert (thus creating a St Budeaux Ferry Road-Saltash single line section) and the 'Down' loop was taken out of use on 2 July 1973 when the Plymouth Panel Signal Box took control of the area. Despite the growth, the view is similar with features such as the 250-and-three-quarter-milepost, the curve of the line and some of the background houses. 43080 front with 43088 out of sight on the rear head for Cornwall with 1C82 1206 London Paddington-Penzance. A glance towards the rear of the train reveals the bend where we saw 47 439 on the vans. Observation of the mini jungle now present there will explain just how difficult it would be now to update that particular scene. *21 April 2015*

This was the second signal box here, replacing the one which had opened on 23 February 1902. It was second hand, redundant from Hatherley Junction, Cheltenham, and opened on 28 June 1908 with a 15-lever frame. A new 25-lever frame was installed in 1952 when the box took over the duties of St Budeaux West Signal Box. It was closed on 2 July 1973 when the Plymouth Panel took over the area. It was an extremely busy signal box as the section of line from here over the Royal Albert Bridge was single line, controlled by the familiar electric train token. This was replaced by a rarely used but most efficient system for a short and busy stretch of single line from 10 July 1961. Putting it in simple layman's terms, both Royal Albert and Saltash Signal Boxes had a 'King' lever. This was an interlocking lever which not only locked with the 'Down' starting signal for Royal Albert, but also electrically locked with the corresponding 'King' lever in Saltash Signal Box. Similarly the Saltash signalman could not pull off his corresponding 'Up' starting signal unless he had pulled his 'King' lever. Thus only the signalman who had pulled the 'King' lever could allow a train on to the bridge. Despite the section being single line, normal 'Up' and 'Down' double line block instruments and bells were used. The line over the bridge was track circuited throughout thus preventing the interlocking levers from being moved whilst a train was in the section.

A close up view of the signal box. The then much younger author pays a visit. Note the fire buckets on the signal box steps. *22 June 1973*

Below left is my picture showing part of the 25-lever frame along with the block shelf with its block instruments and block bells. The 'King' lever was number 20 and is behind the photographer. This system of train working was also used from September to December, in both 1968 and 1970, between Keyham and St Budeaux Ferry Road when the line was temporarily singled for repairs to Weston Mill Viaduct. *22 June 1973*

We can have a study of the layout and arrangements by looking at Ron Andrew's picture, below, of the signal box diagram with the 'Up' and 'Down' block instruments and bells beneath on the block shelf. *Undated 1973*

ROYAL ALBERT, THE AUTO TRAIN ERA

Time was when the view from the Normandy Way overbridge looking towards the two bridges, with Royal Albert Bridge Signal Box to the right, was indeed a very pleasant one. Our first call here is the era of the auto (push-pull) suburban service.

A splendid image supplied by Saltash Heritage Centre originally from my good friend and fellow railway photographer Peter Gray. The 1230 Doublebois-Plymouth in 'sandwich' formation makes its way off the railway bridge. Great changes were on the horizon, the first evidence of which is to the right – the rising Devon-side tower for the Tamar Road Bridge, on which work had commenced the previous year. The auto trains would be replaced (mostly) by Diesel Multiple Units in June 1961. *16 April 1960*

What a difference a couple of years can make! The obvious change to the scene is the addition of the Tamar Road Bridge, opened in October 1961, which was at the time the longest suspension bridge in the country. To the left the battered caravan has gone to meet its maker. On the railway, the wooden foot crossing and the single line token pick up catcher have been removed; the reason for this will be explained when we visit the signal box. 6430 propels the 1235 Plymouth-Saltash, by this time the majority of Saltash suburban services were DMUs. Normal practice for steam was for the engine to pull coaches out to Saltash and propel back. This working formed the 1325 Saltash-Tavistock South, so the engine faced Tavistock, as per normal branch working, and would cease at the year's end, bringing a close to steam working of auto trains over the Royal Albert Bridge. *AC/BM Collection, 7 September 1962*

Moving on a decade and we see changes to the railway scene. The line to St Budeaux was singled on 2 July 1973 when the Plymouth Panel took over. The redundant track which was the former 'Down' main line has yet to be lifted and is quietly rusting away. The other major change is the removal of the semaphore signals which always made such a difference to the working railway scene. A very rare visitor in the shape of the prototype High Speed Train 252 001, on what I believe was its first and only visit to Cornwall, makes its way off the railway bridge. *March 1975*

It is not such a pleasant view now from the Normandy Way overbridge and there have been a substantial number of changes in the intervening years. Railway-wise the reduction to a single track is the most obvious. The combination of growth and a new house detract from the scene. The former signal box remains in use as a Network Rail Office. The road bridge underwent substantial change, completed in 2001, when it became the first suspension bridge in the world to be widened by the addition of two cantilever lanes either side of the central span. We see the south facing one which has altered the appearance of the structure, and there is a lot more traffic on the road bridge as well. 43005 leads with 43182 on the rear with 1A89 1303 Penzance-London Paddington. *21 April 2015*

THE ROYAL ALBERT BRIDGE BY NIGHT

Much has been written elsewhere about this iconic structure. Opened by Prince Albert along with the Cornwall Railway main line from Plymouth to Truro on 2 May 1859, it was without doubt the crowning glory of the Cornwall Railway. Its construction did have one side effect on Saltash and that was the ending of its oyster trade. Environmental considerations were not high on the agenda in the 1840s when construction of the bridge began.

To celebrate its centenary in 1959, the bridge was floodlit. One feature which made this so striking was that it really stood out in the night sky as it stood alone, construction of the Tamar Road Bridge was then in its early stages. The switch for the lights was placed in Royal Albert Bridge Signal Box, and one of the regular signalmen there, Jock Gow, had to be reminded by Saltash station staff on more than one occasion, to turn the lights on as the gathering crowd stood in darkness! This view is from Normandy Way further down the hill from the road bridge. Sadly the angle would not be possible now due to buildings and growth. *June 1959*

Fifty years later the bridge was not floodlit, but celebrations to mark its 150th anniversary were marked with a spectacular firework display, set off from the road bridge, which did not exist half a century earlier. This spectacular view of both bridges and a colourful River Tamar was taken from Saltash Passage and was my first real venture into digital photography for noteworthy events. I suspect Mr Brunel would have approved. We stay on Saltash Passage (in daylight!) for the next couple of pages to have a look at the changing scene here over the years. *2 May 2009*

An unidentified and as yet unnamed Class 50 diesel heads over the Devon land spans of the Royal Albert Bridge with a morning Penzance-Plymouth local service. Standing just to the right of the trees beneath the central land span, we can pick out the number 6 bus waiting to leave for Mount Batten. This is also the point where Wolseley Road finally ends after its long course from Milehouse. *March 1978*

At first glance the scene looks very much the same, there are however some subtle changes. The trees in the 1978 picture and adjoining children's play park are no more. The cluster of buildings on the water front remain but all now bear a different colour scheme; the central one is the much recommended Royal Albert Bridge Inn, two new houses have sprouted to its left. The D Day Memorial on Saltash Passage to the far right has become more prominent with some tidying up of the surrounding site with the Stars and Stripes and the Union Jack flying side by side. The other changes are of course to the road bridge; the effects of the work completed in 2001 by adding of the cantilevers and associated cable work are clearly evident. One feature common to both pictures is the pier behind both bridges which still serves RNAD Ernesettle. 46100 "Royal Scot" makes regal progress over Saltash Passage with 1Z86 1006 Penzance-Bristol Temple Meads "Great Britain" Rail Tour. *27 April 2016*

THE SALTASH FERRY

A slight diversion 'off the rails' to recall a feature once familiar to passengers looking down upon the River Tamar from the Royal Albert Bridge. Still fondly recalled by many local people and with a long history, as it pre-dated the railway passage of the Tamar by a millennia, this was the Saltash Ferry. Whilst a detailed history of it is beyond the scope of this book, the river crossing had been established by the time of the Norman Conquest, its operation ceded to various operators. The ferry rights were granted to Saltash Corporation by Queen Elizabeth I and in the reign of Queen Elizabeth II Saltash surrendered these rights when the ferry was superseded by the Tamar Road Bridge.

In the final days of operation the ferry arrives at Saltash Passage with a veritable selection of classic early 1960s vehicles on display. The road bridge is almost ready for opening. *October 1961*

The Saltash Ferry had two craft with only one in use at a time, the other standing spare and moored up at Saltash Passage on the Devon side of the river. One was sold to a scrap merchant in Ireland but unfortunately sank while being towed on the journey. The other was purchased for use on the King Harry Ferry which traverses the River Fal at Carrick Roads. Converted from steam to diesel operation, new wheel houses fitted on the upper deck, new gates and a lick of paint, the floating bridge still had that 'Saltash look'. It served here for about a decade, and then unfortunately also sank whilst on tow to the scrapyard! *30 April 1969*

Whereas the main spans of both the bridges at Saltash cross the Tamar in a straight line, the course of the ferry was at an angle, clearly evident in this view taken from Saltash pier in the last week of operation. We are looking over the river towards Saltash Passage with both bridges to the left, the road bridge still carrying its catwalk used in construction, the ferry setting off with a healthy complement of traffic. The Ferry ceased running on 23 October 1961 with the road bridge opening the following day. *October 1961*

The present-day view is taken from the former ferry slipway, where pleasure craft now come and go. The view over the Tamar towards Saltash Passage has not changed that much, other than the by growth, the skyline and the houses look much the same. The two bridges stand aloft, the railway one with its fresh coat of paint, after a three year restoration scheme by Network Rail, the road one with its catwalk removed and then later extended by the cantilevers of 2001. The slipway directly opposite on the Devon shore was used by American Forces in World War II. Many personnel left for D Day and other allied operations, their sacrifices commemorated by an appropriate memorial on Saltash Passage, mentioned earlier, indeed we will remember them. Reminders of the ferry service survive, in particular the former slipways on both sides of the river. Adjacent to the one at Saltash Passage, one can still sample the delights of the Ferry House Inn, where I suspect many a pint was enjoyed while waiting for the ferry. *21 April 2015*

A LOOK AT ONE BRIDGE FROM ANOTHER

A unique picture, taken from the Tamar Road Bridge on its opening day by my good friend Colin Lennox-Jones, 1021 'County of Montgomery' heads west with a Penzance-bound train. Nicely framed in the piers of the railway bridge is the Saltash Ferry; moored up having been made redundant the previous day. *24 October 1961*

The best view of the railway bridge from the road bridge is to be had on a summer evening, as we see top right. D1058 'Western Nobleman' with 1B83 1530 London Paddington-Penzance evokes memories of the Diesel Hydraulic era. On the foreshore stands the old custom house, now a private residence. The view today is basically unchanged. *13 June 1974*

The inscription 'IK BRUNEL ENGINEER' was placed on either end of the main spans by the directors of the Cornwall Railway as a tribute shortly after his death. The lettering was installed by Plymouth Iron founders, who tendered £15.00 for the contract. Steam on a summer evening here is not a common sight nowadays. This is 76 079 on the rear of a return excursion 1Z22 1805 Carne Point-Plymouth. *29 May 2006*

After earlier mentioning a hostelry that served many a traveller crossing the Tamar by ferry, now a visit to one that has served many a rail passenger (and railwayman!) crossing the Tamar by train. I refer to the pub opposite Saltash Station

To the far right D1009 'Western Invader' waits patiently as 4M05 1205 Penzance-Crewe is loaded with the produce of the Tamar Valley, an operation at certain times of the year that could take up to 20 minutes. To the left, situated on the very steep Albert Road, is the Royal Albert Bridge Hotel. Its namesake is clearly visible behind, and clearly legible beneath the then pub name is the now historic legend 'The Plymouth Breweries Ltd', an inscription once so common on pubs in the area, and one fondly recalled by many who enjoyed their superb best bitter. *August 1966*

Like the railways, the changes within the pub and brewing industry have been many over the last half century and are beyond the scope of this book. Suffice to say Plymouth Breweries were taken over by Courage South West in 1970 and the majority of affected pubs passed to Ushers of Trowbridge in 1995. It is in Ushers livery we see the renamed (date unknown) pub, now The Two Bridges. Other than a tree growing up behind the telegraph pole opposite the pub, little else has changed. *February 2001*

The pub now does not show allegiance to any brewery as it is now privately owned which is reflected by the changed inn sign and a further lick of paint. The basic view is still very recognisable. The pub has gained a satellite TV dish and the pole opposite has remained constant, but look how that sapling in the beer garden (where I once enjoyed many a pint) has grown to virtually obliterate the view of the two bridges. Surprisingly the tree behind the telegraph pole has vanished. *9 September 2015*

SALTASH STATION LOOKING WEST

D1030 'Western Musketeer' stands waiting to reverse into the goods yard to pick up milk tanks. To the right is the 'Up' platform with its stone building dating from the 1880 station rebuilding, and extended in the early 1900s due to the boom in suburban traffic. To the left is the waiting shelter on the 'Down' platform. Behind stands the footbridge, provided circa 1909, with its dual exit to the 'Up' platform and Station Hill. Saltash Baptist Church keeps watch from Culver Road. *21 June 1969*

Another light engine movement stands at the 'Up' platform, this time HST power cars 43030 + 43163, the latter carrying Plymouth Ocean City advertising livery, running as 0Z77 1145 Penzance-Laira having rescued the 'Down' Paddington-Penzance sleeper from Par earlier in the day. The changes are many both on and off the rails. The upside building was sold out of railway use a long time ago. It has lost its canopy and looks very forlorn. The footbridge was demolished on 9 April 1989; the church was burnt down on Christmas Day 1987 to be replaced by a new building that opened in March1992, but growth now obscures its outlook over the station. Notice how the house to the far right has gained an attractive extension to its roof. In the next couple of pages we will study both outside and inside that once proud upside building in happier times. *5 September 2015*

THE ANATOMY OF A WAYSIDE STATION

Promotion, in October 1965, took me from the Parcels Office at Plymouth Station to the post of Area Relief Clerk, covering from Devonport to Bodmin Road (it was not a Parkway then), including Looe, Bere Alston and Tavistock North, with my home station being Saltash. This is where I learnt my trade as a railway clerk and Jim Lewis, who went on to become a great personal friend, taught me everything I knew. Saltash was still a busy place in 1965 with a steady passenger flow, fruit and flower traffic plus milk, of which more later. My stay of just under five years there holds many special memories. In this and the next few pages let me take you through how a wayside station worked, the hub being the building on the 'Up' platform which we see in a far more presentable condition than it is now.

The expression 'you cannot see the wood for the trees' takes on a whole new meaning on the Friday before Mothering Sunday as the 1215 Saltash to Newcastle 'flower special' is being loaded, the platform covered by a sea of fresh flower boxes – just look at the sheer volume. There was also a heavy flow to the London markets. I recall some of the destinations for northern traffic; TJ Poupart of Liverpool, Bradnum's of Hull. The flower traffic was seasonal, starting in earnest in February, peaking March-April and then decreasing as summer approached. Strawberries, the best fruit, peaked in June to mid-July. Fruit and flowers were brought in daily from the Callington/Harrowbarrow/St Dominic/Cargreen area by Fred Rogers Ltd of St Dominic. This road haulier worked for the railway as an agent and handled the accounts for some of the growers. This was a long-standing agreement which had its origins in the GWR, ensuring the market produce from that part of the valley came to Saltash as opposed to the SR at Callington, Gunnislake or Calstock. All this was very much in the pre-digital age: it was the era of carbon copies. The flower accounts had to be done in triplicate, one for the sender, one for our head office in Plymouth and one held at the station. Consignment notes had to be prepared in duplicate, and we also issued a memo-waybill to accompany each individual consignment. All copies had to be legible and the blue stain of the carbon paper would remain on one's hands for days. It was very hard to wash off, and it was all over one's shirt causing mother much consternation. Rationalisation of this traffic in 1967 heralded its decline and what was left either came into Plymouth or went over to the road hauliers in a very short space of time. *18 March 1966*

THE ANATOMY OF A WAYSIDE STATION

We pay a visit to the booking office. Saltash was the first station in the area to see mechanisation when the mini-printer was installed in 1955. This is the green machine seen on the counter. Until the opening of the Tamar Road Bridge in October 1961, suburban traffic was heavy and the station saw 1,000 passengers daily before 0830. The mini printer issued single or day returns, adult or child, with three destination options; St Budeaux, Keyham Dockyard Halt Devonport and Plymouth. On my first day here Jim Lewis inducted me to ticket-issuing procedures, demonstrating by booking the 1020 local service. I was told it was just here mostly a matter of pressing the right button for the mini-printer. A single to St Budeaux, a couple of day returns to Plymouth and then Jim invited me to take the reins – and the next person requested a first class return to Newcastle via London. Talk about a baptism of fire! The large ticket rack had printed stock for a wide range of destinations both locally and beyond, including tickets routed via Okehampton for the SR route valid via Plymouth. Twelve issues a year was the minimum requirement for printed stock. One lady travelled monthly to Tipton Owen Street in the West Midlands to see her mother – one of the more unusual travel flows. Passenger traffic fell away sharply due to a combination of local day-return fares being massively increased in June 1966 and train service reductions not long afterwards. The station was unstaffed from October 1971. I have sat at that table in the foreground with three other clerks processing the flower traffic whilst a further colleague manned the booking window – a veritable hive of industry. Now there is just silence. *January 1966*

Signalman John Thomas leans out of the signal box, a member of the Permanent Way gang surveys some wooden rail blocks and D843 'Sharpshooter' waits in the 'Up' platform before going into the yard to collect the milk tanks. It had been a fairly recent innovation to despatch an engine to Saltash to collect the tanks for the 1350 St Erth-Kensington milk for attachment at Plymouth. This was to save blocking the 'Up' main line at a busy time of day. *10 October 1969*

We can pay a visit to the signal box and take a look at the diagram, a fine image supplied by Ron Andrews, at the time a relief signalman in the area. Saltash Signal Box was equipped with a 31-lever frame. Number 25 was the 'King' lever for working the single line with Royal Albert Box. The diagram nicely shows the double track from the west and the single line over the bridge. Close examination reveals that the 'Down' platform was signalled for a train from Plymouth to terminate here and simply reverse for the return journey. *Undated circa 1972/3*

The 'King' lever is nicely illustrated as we study the west end of the frame. It is the one painted half blue and brown and has been pulled giving Saltash permission to despatch a train over the bridge. The short handle is an indication that it operated electrically controlled equipment. The signalman is Ken Lay, who went on to become an Assistant Area Manager at Plymouth and was another good friend. The box closed when the Plymouth Panel took control of the area on 2 July 1973 and it is the signalman there who now decides the priority of trains over the rail bridge. *January 1968*

SALTASH GOODS YARD

Saltash Goods Yard, situated between the wall of the Baptist churchyard and Coombe-By-Saltash Viaduct, was a rather cramped affair tucked away to the west side of the station. It was opened in 1880 as part of the station rebuilding. Formerly there was a goods siding behind the 'Up' platform, this being removed and infilled to provide for the extension of the station building and the signal box we have visited.

The view from Culver Road as D1050 'Western Ruler' heads past with 1A43 0915 Penzance-London Paddington. The goods yard with a typical GWR goods shed is to the right, to its left are two circular sheds, one painted white, the other green, which formerly served as the GWR bus garage. In the yard to the right of the coal wagon are the milk tanks being loaded. Saltash despatched up to five 2,000 gallon capacity milk tanks a day to London at £300 a time. Destinations varied according to the requirements of the Milk Marketing Board and were mainly; West Ealing, Cricklewood, Morden, Wandsworth Road and Ilford. The milk of course had to be consigned and billed daily, and a lengthy account was sent monthly – all this of course involved more carbon paper for the clerks – to Unigate Creameries, By The Sea Road, Trowbridge, Wilts. I never did discover how Trowbridge had a road by the sea! The milk was brought up by road tankers from Dawes Creamery on the Waterfront situated just by the base pier of the road bridge. Changing markets for milk meant this traffic ceased at Saltash circa 1970 and the creamery itself closed in 1973. *9 October 1969*

A much changed view today as Voyager 220 033 passes by with 1M49 0940 Penzance-Manchester Piccadilly. The goods yard finally closed in October 1971 when the station became unstaffed, and was disconnected in October 1972, the rails were lifted the following year. Subsequent housing development has the seen the yard eradicated and of course there is the inevitable growth to complete the changing scene. *21 April 2015*

We turn around to look the other way from Culver Road, although this picture was actually taken from the former footbridge which at the time hindered the view from the road bridge. It shows the station when it was still in its prime and kept neat and tidy, the staff took pride in the floral displays and it was a worthy gateway to Cornwall. Entering the station is D603 'Cossack' with 1V33 0702 Bradford Forster Square-Penzance, the 'Down' 'Cornishman'. *June 1966*

With the footbridge demolished, the updated image is taken a few yards further back from Culver Road. At first glance the overall scene is very similar but there are changes, those to the road bridge having already been noted. The station building was sold off many years ago to the local council, and then to a developer. Sadly this is now an eyesore and something local people wish to address. Its replacement welcome shelter is built on the site of the former signal box which in turn was built on the site of the former 'Up' siding. The Friends of Saltash Station volunteers do a wonderful job of keeping the station neat and tidy with gardens the former staff would have been proud of. The larger building behind the waiting shelter on the down platform is the relay room for Plymouth Panel. 150 246 calls with 2C47 1349 Plymouth-Penzance and this completes our look at the GWR system on the west side of Plymouth. Now we take a walk onto the road bridge, where we look down and make our acquaintance with that other railway which served the City. The Southern beckons. *21 April 2015*

THE SOUTHERN ROUTE

While there was much rivalry between the two railways, I think my old friend Russell Leitch put matters in context when he wrote in his book on Plymouth's Railways in the 1930s (published by the RCTS) that without a doubt, the Southern was the poor relation in Plymouth. It could only reach its own terminus at Friary by running powers from Devonport Junction to Friary Junction and, at times, to the tune of the GWR who tended to give their trains priority if there was congestion on the eastern side of North Road Station.

Like the Great Western, the Southern also entered the City from the east, but on its northern flank, coming in 'through the back door'. Crossing the boundary at Tamerton, the route then came down the reclaimed south bank of the Tamar where from the Tamar Road Bridge we see rebuilt Bulleid Pacific 34058 'Sir Frederick Pile' with the 1125 Brighton-Plymouth passing the RNAD Ernesettle Armaments Depot, constructed between 1922 and 1926, with its still-extant pier to the left and former internal narrow gauge railway system seen curving away to the right. *9 October 1963*

Moving on by 14 years the view is unchanged, save for what was a double track main line is now a single track branch line, St Budeaux to Bere Alston being singled on 7 September 1970. 33 104 leads the Thames-Tamar Rail Tour back from Bere Alston on its way to London Waterloo via Friary. Since the creation of what is now the St Budeaux-Gunnislake Branch, locomotives are a rare sight on this stretch of line. *16 April 1977*

Other than some growth, the view is basically unchanged today, but taking a picture of it is difficult since the addition of the east side cantilever to the road bridge has meant there is no pedestrian access. The narrow-gauge railway system within the RNAD Depot ceased working when displaced by road transport early in 1980 and the rails were lifted later the same year. An unidentified Class 150 Sprinter heads for Plymouth on 2B14 1905 Gunnislake-Plymouth. *23 September 1993*

Before we leave the Tamar Road Bridge, here are some memories of a time-honoured train that ran over the SR route for many years. The train schedules of today bear no relation to those of fifty years ago and this is one facet where things have changed for the better. As late as 1964, the last weekday service from Plymouth to Paddington was at 1630. Miss that to get to London and it would be a long wait for the sleeper, unless one was brave enough to use the 1652 to Eastleigh, which remarkably survived to be diesel hauled until it finally ran in March 1967. Other than Tamerton Foliot (closed in September 1962) and Bere Ferrers, the train called at every station between Plymouth and Exeter Central. Devonport Albert Road, Dockyard Halt and Keyham replaced the Devonport Kings Road and Ford stops after the SR route through Camels Head had closed, arriving at Exeter Central at 1923. After a 32-minute wait a 1955 departure ensued and, other than St James' Park Halt, Sutton Bingham, Dinton and Wilton South, the train called at all stations to Salisbury arriving at 2252 and departing at 2310 for Eastleigh arriving at 2346. A long layover then ensued as the train was then attached to the 2213 Weymouth Mail which, after a leisurely journey through Thomas Hardy's Wessex, arrived at 0120 to pick up the Plymouth portion leaving at 0126. Further calls in the middle of the night at Winchester, Basingstoke, Farnborough Main, Woking, Weybridge and Surbiton brought the weary traveller into London Waterloo at 0348, just under 11 hours after leaving Plymouth and having called at 41 intermediate stations. I wonder how many passengers stayed the full course! The train conveyed the return newspaper vans off the down overnight 0110 from Waterloo, and it was a busy parcel and mail service. From Bere Alston it carried Tamar Valley flowers/fruit for the London markets. I have traced the train as far back as the 1932 timetable, and it certainly ran before that, where it is shown as the 1648 Ilfracombe to Eastleigh with the Plymouth-Exeter section shown as a separate train, otherwise the timings remained identical. We see the train heading away from the City in its penultimate week of operation hauled by an unidentified Class 42 'Warship' with the vans on the rear. For the record, the last steam locomotive to haul the train from Plymouth to Exeter was Standard 5 number 73 030 on 5 September 1964. Two days later the departure time from Plymouth was advanced by two minutes to accommodate the extra stop at Dockyard Halt. A direct service from Dockyard Halt to leafy Weybridge takes some imagination!

The train made its final run on 4 March 1967. *February 1967*

ST BUDEAUX VICTORIA ROAD

St Budeaux Victoria Road is the only remaining former Southern Railway Station still open for passengers in the City of Plymouth. Opened with the route from Lydford to Devonport on 2 June 1890, the station served the growing suburbs in this part of north-west Plymouth, and a number of the direct trains to and from Waterloo called right up until their demise in 1964. The suffix 'Victoria Road' was added from 26 September 1949. Upon closure of the route from Bere Alston to Okehampton, in May 1968, the station became part of the newly created Gunnislake Branch. The track was singled in 1970.

From the camera of my good friend Terry Nicholls, re-built 'Battle of Britain' Class 34090 'Sir Eustace Missenden', Southern Railway arrives with the Sunday 1015 Exeter Central-Plymouth. The image does convey this as a well kept main line with a typical Southern upper quadrant signal, the name-board painted in chocolate and cream, a reminder that the Western Region had control of commercial, but not operating matters, of the SR system west of Exeter from 1952 to 1958. *July 1963*

Locomotives are now a rare sight in the station, 37 604 pauses with 37 295 on the rear with 1Q13 Network Rail Radio test train. Only the curve of the platform suggests any link with the top picture, the station now an untidy, unstaffed halt on the single line branch and substantial growth blocks any view of the houses in Pemros Road behind. *3 May 2012*

Railway rivalry took various forms, especially where two systems ran in very close proximity with an adjacent or even shared station. It was not unusual for one or either to do its best to ignore the other. Such was the case here. When the station opened in 1890 it was advertised as 'St Budeaux for Saltash', for passengers to make their way to Saltash Passage for the ferry across the Tamar. The Great Western opened its adjacent St Budeaux Station on 1 June 1904. Thus despite there being a GWR station literally alongside with a frequent train service to Saltash, the LSWR and later the SR still advised their passengers to alight here and take a bus, or taxi, or walk to Saltash Passage for the Ferry. Common sense only really came with Nationalisation in 1948.

A general view of the station looking towards Okehampton, showing the principal buildings were on the 'Down', Plymouth-bound platform and particularly noteworthy to the right is the archway, a remnant of the covered walkway which led up to Wolseley Road. *July 1966*

A higher elevation view showing how the station has changed, and not for the better. The abandoned and deserted former 'Down' platform really says it all as we observe a very unusual visitor to the Gunnislake Branch in the form of 58 031 on a clearance test run to Ernesettle Sidings. Common to both pictures are the houses behind the station in Pemros Road. Other than further growth hindering the view this scene is little changed today. *27 March 2002*

ST BUDEAUX FROM CARDINAL AVENUE

Here we have a magnificent panorama of St Budeaux and its railways from my good friend Terry Nicholls. Taken from Cardinal Avenue, there is so much to absorb in this photograph it is difficult to know where to start. So let us begin with the train, the 0730 Yeoford-Friary goods (due at Friary at 1315) hauled by un-rebuilt 'West Country' Pacific 34023 'Blackmore Vale'. The engine is preserved by the Bulleid Preservation Society and is currently based and operating on the Bluebell Railway which runs along the border between East and West Sussex. The load of three goods brake vans and one parcel van was hardly economic for a light Pacific, and it was this sort of train that was coming under the scrutiny of Dr Beeching around this time. The train is on the former Southern main line heading for Devonport Kings Road via Weston Mill. Immediately behind it are the former 'Up' SR sidings then still retained for engineering use, which lead the eye to the wartime connection between the two systems opened on 21 March 1941.

The GWR main line is to the far left leading to St Budeaux Ferry Road Station. St Budeaux Victoria Road Station is to the right behind the SR arch under Wolseley Road, in front of which stands the SR Signal Box closed on 25 July 1965. Notice the flat roof of Victoria Road Signal Box, an out of character and hurried replacement for bomb damage inflicted in April 1941. To the far right is the SR goods shed and yard which closed on 11 December 1961. In the far background the two bridges at Saltash are clearly visible. This picture also doubles as a wonderful street scene of St Budeaux, with St Budeaux Square to the far right, behind which stands St Paul's RC Church providing a notable landmark. Also worthy of note is the amount of vehicular traffic on the road, bearing in mind that at the time this was the main road access route from the City Centre towards the Tamar Road Bridge. *15 June 1963*

(OPPOSITE PAGE, TOP) Moving on a couple of decades, the view is still very recognisable. The major changes are on the rails, with the eradication of the former SR route towards Weston Mill and the former 'Up' SR sidings, and a garage prominent where we saw 34023. All mechanical signalling vanished on 2 July 1973 when the Plymouth Panel took over control of the area. The wartime link between the two systems is now the start of the single line Gunnislake Branch, where we see 08 377 heading for Ernesettle RNAD with the transfer goods, its load now reduced to only warrant a Class 08 shunting engine. It would finish completely two years later. Look just beyond the 08 and the neat allotments between the two systems have become a grassy wasteland. The road has been widened, the new, expanded dual carriageway, invading the former SR goods yard, had opened on 6 October 1971. St Pauls RC Church and the two bridges at Saltash still act as good landmarks. *17 June 1982*

Moving on by three decades, and a few yards to the right, due to access and growth problems, we see substantial changes, background landmarks such as St Pauls RC Church and the two bridges at Saltash confirm the location. As for the railways, they are hardly visible amongst the developments of the former railway land and the growth. Look to the far left, just beyond the new Lidl store, for a glimpse of Ferry Road Station. To its right, in the short gap between that and the St Budeaux Community Centre, the cab of 150 249 working 2G74 1054 Plymouth-Gunnislake can just be seen exactly where we see 08 377 in the top picture, some precision timing required to press the shutter for this one. Yes the two trains really are in the same place. The former allotments have become a mini forest. The main road has seen layout and marking alterations, the mini roundabout and the inevitable bus lanes effectively turn it back to a single carriageway, and again there is a surprising lack of traffic! Here we have a place where both the City and the Railways have seen their own evolving change of scene. *21 April 2015*

ST BUDEAUX SIDINGS

Another splendid picture from Terry Nicholls, this one taken from the Western Region St Budeaux Ferry Road Signal Box, which we have previously visited, as 'N' Class 31838 pulls away from St Budeaux Victoria Road towards Weston Mill past the empty SR engineering sidings with the Sunday 1015 Exeter Central-Plymouth. Many a signalman working in the Western Region Signal Box found it strange to have trains running behind their signal box, and usually with a friendly wave from the footplate, over which they had no control as these were, of course, covered by the Southern Victoria Road Signal Box. *15 December 1963*

Due to the demolition of the former St Budeaux Ferry Road Signal Box and access problems to its site, the view point has moved a few yards west and to the other side of the track to the footpath which runs down from Wolseley Road. Two decades on and we see another train leaving Victoria Road for Plymouth, in this case the rare sight of a Class 37 coming off the Gunnislake Branch on a passenger train. 37 182 leads with 37 185 rear with the 1625 Bere Alston-Paddington via Friary and Heathfield leg of 'The Goonbarrow Belle' Rail Tour. The train will pass in front of the former signal box as opposed to behind it. This view is now impossible due to the construction of a St Budeaux version of the Berlin Wall beside the footpath, and as can be ascertained from the high level view from Cardinal Avenue, the view looking towards St Budeaux Square would be very different. *3 March 1984*

We have already seen this view from afar as we explored the footpath that led off Weston Mill Viaduct towards St Budeaux. Between St Budeaux Victoria Road and Ford, the former SR line crossed Wolseley Road by two masonry arches. This is the first of them, a substantial structure, and the rising gradient of the line towards Weston Mill is very noticeable. In those pre-metric days the motorist is advised of the 14-foot height restriction. *August 1965*

There is no trace whatsoever of the masonry arch which once ook the Southern main line over Wolseley Road at this point. Looking beyond where the arch once stood the retaining wall running down from Fletemoor Road, which is directly under Cardinal Avenue where we enjoyed the changing view from above, is still there although it has changed colour. The curve of the road is further confirmation of the location; the modern day lamppost to the left is almost in the identical position to its predecessor. *19 April 2015*

WESTON MILL HALT

A train we have already discussed, the 'Eastleigh', is seen here in its final week of steam haulage with 'West Country' Class 34107 'Blandford Forum' passing the site of the former Weston Mill Halt. Opened on 1 November 1906 as the LSWR suburban service was growing, the station was short-lived, closing in September 1921. No known photograph of it exists. It was the LSWR which was the first to make provision for mainline suburban traffic in the City in the 1890s, several locals running purely from Devonport to St Budeaux. One of them was progressively timed earlier as the autumn evenings darkened and correspondingly later as the spring evenings lengthened, because the Dockyard could then only work in daylight. How that situation has changed! *August 1964 published courtesy of Colour Rail*

The view point is the same and, allowing for the expected growth, there are many similarities between the two images. For example the Terrace on the right has seen only the colour of the houses change, beyond we can still see Camel's Head School, to the far right an enlarged Wolseley Road and the general back drop of the houses of Weston Mill remain constant. It is the railway that has changed; quite simply it has been eradicated beyond all trace. *6 November 2011*

The viewpoint has changed to the other side of the line and the photographer, Terry Nicholls, was standing slightly further towards the iron span which took the railway over Ferndale Road. When opened in 1890 it crossed the open waters of Camel's Head Creek. 'Battle of Britain' 34062 '17 Squadron' working the Sunday 1500 Plymouth-London Waterloo is midway between two former stations, for just on the south side of the span was the former Camel's Head Halt, opened with Weston Mill Halt on 1 November 1906 but lasting much longer – until 4 May 1942. This is probably the shortest distance between two stations in the City, an example of the intensity of the suburban services at their short-lived peak for the first two decades of the last century. On the following page we shall observe this embankment with a train heading towards Plymouth. *10 November 1963*

For a higher and more distant perspective of this changing scene, we return to Poole Park Road for a view of Class 42 'Warship' D829 'Magpie' heading towards Weston Mill Viaduct with 3B30 1330 Penzance-Bristol vans, the leading one a truly magnificent former LNER specimen. In the right hand background the track bed of the former SR route with the metal span over Ferndale Road between the two halts is clearly visible. This view is impossible today due to growth. If it were, it would look very different as the SR line has been completely eradicated, the road under the metal span is now the St Budeaux Bypass, with a new junction and traffic lights controlling the Ferndale Road Junction, which is very familiar to many a motorist especially at peak times. The fire station concrete tower would be a good link as that is still in use. *8 June 1968*

WESTON MILL AND CAMEL'S HEAD

With thanks to another old friend, Sid Sponheimer, we view the embankment between Weston Mill and Camel's Head Halts from another perspective, that of Wolseley Road and its prefabs, the latter at the time still in plentiful supply in many parts of the City. 34002 'Salisbury' heads towards Devonport with 1V71 1130 Brighton-Plymouth and is approaching the former metal bridge over Carlton Terrace. The motor cycle has just turned right to pass beneath it. Look towards the rear of the train and just behind the Atlantean Bus, on what was then a two-lane road, is the former tram shed. *26 August 1964*

To the right, this is now the start of the A3064 St Budeaux Bypass of circa 1988 and, to the left, the main entrance point to the Naval Base. The former two-lane road now has four lanes. The prefabs have been swept away and replaced by more modern housing. Of the railway little remains save for a small part of the embankment visible in the distance beyond the traffic light. It is the background which is the best link between the two images, with one notable difference. Look to the top right of 34 002 in the top picture and St Phillips Church in Bridwell road is prominent. This was demolished in April 2014 due to major problems of water ingress and damp, now replaced by the shining white new housing on its site. The organ in St Phillips was dismantled by organ-builder firm Michael Farley and rebuilt in Cornwood Church. My wife was part of that team and informed me she could have just told me the date and saved me all the time researching the demise of the church. It is a small world sometimes. The world gets even smaller! When I was relating the story down at the local pub one of my drinking companions, Geoff Henderson, informed me that his son Jamie's first job as an architect involved the design of the affordable housing and flats that replaced St Phillips Church. *11 January 2016*

An alternative title for this pairing of pictures would be 'the railway passing through Camel's Head by Wordsworth Road'. The 52 years between them tell the story of a scene which can best be described as having changed dramatically.

A fine shot by Terry Nicholls showing the well-maintained SR main line as 34090, in charge of the Sunday 1500 Plymouth-London Waterloo, speeds along between Ford (Devon) and St Budeaux, passing the Victoria Road 'Up' distant signal. In simple layman's terms, a distant signal is not a stop signal; it is an indication when in the 'off' position as in this case that the driver has a clear road ahead with all stop signals clear for the next block section. If it were in the 'on' position, it would be a warning to be prepared to stop at the first signal. Back to the matters in hand, the train has just crossed the second bridge over Wolseley Road. To the left is the pleasure park still in use with the houses of Cookworthy Road behind. More than likely this is the same day as we saw 34090 arriving at Victoria Road. The Exmouth Junction (Exeter) crew worked down with the Sunday 1015 from Exeter Central and returned with the same engine on the 1500 from Plymouth. *July 1963*

Yes this really is the same spot, and there is a link between the two images – the houses to the very top right background of each picture. There is no evidence that a railway once passed through here, but housing development on the route of the line towards Camel's Head sees new streets bearing names such as Bulleid Close, Maunsell Close and Drummond Close. These so named after the designers of the locomotives which once plied their steamy way through here.
19 April 2015

WOSELEY ROAD OVERBRIDGE, SWILLY

The SR route from St Budeaux to Devonport crossed Wolseley Road for the second time by its junction for Cookworthy Road to the left, and Biddick Drive/North Down Crescent to the right. The railway was constructed here on land through the Swilly Estate, a very historic Plymouth Manor. The Swilly housing estate was built in the 1920s as a part of Plymouth's contribution to the provision of homes mainly for former Officers after World War I. The two houses to the left are a classic example of the architecture of the period. The area is now officially known as North Prospect, but to many locals it is still Swilly. Despite the railway line that passed over the arch having been closed almost twelve months and demolition being imminent, this was still a lucrative site for British Transport Advertising as evidenced by the number of hoardings. These were a once a familiar sight over many railway locations in the City, another feature of the changing scene from half a century ago. British Transport Advertising had a small staff based right at the east end of the building on Platform 2 at Plymouth Station and I knew them very well. *August 1965*

The kerb on Cookworthy Road at its junction with Wolseley Road and the houses to the immediate left tells us this is definitely the same location to the inch! The major change of course is the disappearance of the former railway arch and its embankment, allowing for Wolseley Road to be widened creating the dual carriageway we know today. The former Swilly housing estate is undergoing a major regeneration, the bright colours of the houses a reflection of this. There is also a distinct lack of advertising hoardings as British Transport Advertising is no more. We shall now take a short walk up the hill to study the view in the other direction. *19 April 2015*

I have walked up the hill a few yards to present the view of the second Wolseley Road overbridge looking back towards Camel's Head. The Cookworthy Road junction is to the right. In the era of the horse and cart, the single arch was no doubt perfectly adequate when the bridge was built for the 1890 opening of the line. By the early 1960s the arch, and in particular the embankment to the left on the Ford side, was an obstruction on either side of the dual carriageway, for by now this was the main road from the City Centre towards the Tamar Road Bridge. It was an obstacle the City Council would soon remove. British Transport advertising had been hard at work on this side of the bridge as well, telling us, quite forcefully, to enjoy the 'Guinness Sensation'. *August 1965*

As with the view looking up the hill, the removal of both arch and embankment has allowed for the road to be widened, creating the uninterrupted dual carriageway. It has also opened a much clearer view beyond the former arch, and in particular, to the left, revealed one of Plymouth's hidden architectural gems. I am referring to Wolseley Road Flats, built by the City Council in the early 1930s and now transferred to Plymouth Community Homes, a superb example of construction in the inter-war period. The dip in the road here often causes problems when heavy rain produces flash flooding, motorists beware there are a couple of very active speed cameras here! *19 April 2015*

FORD (DEVON)

Ford was given the suffix 'Devon' on 9 July 1923 to distinguish it from Ford 'Sussex'. The daily through train between Plymouth and Brighton in each direction ran through both and called at neither!

A gem from the late RC Sambourne of 'M7' 30035 with an ancient ex LSWR three-coach rake arriving with the 1730 Brentor-Plymouth Friary.

Prominent is the impressive 58-foot-span bridge carrying the inappropriately named 'Brunel Terrace' over the line, and believed to be one of the first such structures in the country to be made from poured concrete. When built in 1890 it carried a country lane to the St Aubyn Estate. *July 1954*

Little has changed almost a decade later as 'N' Class 31 842 passes with the 0730 Yeoford-Friary Goods, a train noted for its mixed stock and number of goods brake vans. The 'N' Class were a familiar sight on the route throughout the Southern Railway and British Railways eras. *Picture courtesy of Dave Down AC/BM Collection, 29 February 1964*

Such has been the complete eradication of the site and infilling of the land that the station has vanished without trace. High above the platforms where the photographers stood and people once waited for their trains, what looks like a wall going across the middle of the picture among the trees is, in fact, the parapet of the Brunel Terrace Bridge; it is such a pity one cannot now study this fine piece of engineering. This really is the same place. The destruction has been total. *6 November 2011*

Ford (Devon), I think is best described as a country station in the city suburbs. When opened in 1890 it was certainly in a more rural area as development of the surrounding lands had yet to start. Like St Budeaux Victoria Road, the main buildings were on the 'Down', Plymouth-bound direction side, the canopy very much in keeping with the standard LSWR design of the time. Bere Ferrers, Brentor, Whitstone and Bridgerule (on the Bude branch) and Corfe Castle in rural Dorset are other notable examples. This view, taken from the 1652 Plymouth-Eastleigh in the last fortnight of the station's life shows a very typical LSWR station, the main buildings hugging the end of the cutting in which the station was partly built. *AC/BM Collection, August 1964*

The 1155 Plymouth-Exeter Central served all intermediate stations, before combining with an Ilfracombe portion at Central to form the 1430 to London Waterloo arriving at 1833. It is seen here running into the station in the charge of D1049 'Western Monarch'. I do recall seeing D1027 'Western Lancer' on this working back in April 1964, just three days after it had set a new Paddington-Plymouth record time in preparation for the introduction of the 'Golden Hind' in June 1964, another example of the versatility of the class. Not all the long distance trains stopped at Ford. The 1155 was another time-honoured train like the 'Eastleigh'. Not the fastest of services to the capital, but it was direct and convenient for intermediate stations. An updated view covering both images will feature on the next page. *August 1964*

FORD (DEVON)

Not one of my better pictures, but views of steam engines coming through Ford from the Brunel Terrace overbridge are hard to come by. 34010 'Sidmouth' hurries through with the 1546 Okehampton-Plymouth, the train by now a connection rather than a 'through' portion off the 1100 from London Waterloo 'Atlantic Coast Express' to Padstow by way of the former North Cornwall line. As from June 1963 the 'through' coaches from the City ran only on Saturdays. This splendid view is looking south, showing the station partially built in a cutting and the superbly engineered line over Ford Viaduct leading to Ford Tunnel. Ford Signal Box, which opened in 1891 and closed on 2 March 1947, was situated to the right just beyond the footbridge. Originally an 11-lever frame with six working and five spare levers, this was extended in 1900 to 14 levers, 13 working with one spare, for a short siding used to unload bricks for the new housing estates. This was installed between the station and the viaduct also on the 'Up', right hand side of the line. Ford had limited freight facilities and these are recorded as being withdrawn from 1 September 1952, although the siding would not have been available for use once the signal box had closed. *July 1964*

Same place, different view as we look across the valley from the block of flats in Cross Hill to see 31 118 about to pass Dockyard Halt on a special conveying the McAlpine private saloons from Cornwall towards Plymouth. In the background we see Ford Viaduct; the two lines winding their way through the western suburbs were never far apart. The Brunel Terrace overbridge looks quite impressive from this distance. Former local landmarks of note are the gasometers to the far right in St Leaven Road. We shall return to Brunel Terrace on the next page. *6 October 1982*

We return to the Brunel Terrace overbridge for the view of the railway through Ford after demolition and before annihilation. Although the station has been wiped off the face of the earth (demolished in the 1970s) and the space between the platforms filled in, the arc of the line over Ford Viaduct to the Pasley Street overbridge and Ford tunnel is still clearly defined. To the top right we can spot Dockyard Halt and the block of flats in Cross Hill where the lower picture on the previous page was taken. At the end of the cutting on the right, we see the houses which mark the start of Station Road, which I have already pointed out was unique with a station at each end, Ford Halt on the Great Western line is but a quarter of a mile down the road. I wonder if this Station Road is still unique now with a closed station at each end. *6 October 1982*

The present-day view from the Brunel Terrace overbridge is as depressing as the weather was on the day I visited. The changes are indeed dramatic, the land has seen further infilling and further substantial house building; the bricks for these were certainly not unloaded in Ford siding! There is no indication a railway, a station and a viaduct ever existed here, and tree growth limits the view over the St Levan Valley. Station Road, out of sight to the right, still links the two former stations. *13 November 2011*

FORD VIADUCT

This graceful structure of seven 50ft spans, 135 yards in length and a maximum height of 88ft, took the SR route from Ford Station over the St Levan Valley towards the twin tunnels which lead to Devonport. The arches were of concrete block construction, but this was not readily evident as the exterior of the viaduct was of dark blue limestone. As in the case of the GWR Keyham Viaduct, at the time the structure was built the local landscape was very different to that of today as the railway crossed a muddy tidal creek.

Lifting of the rails is under way in this view looking back from near the Pasley Street overbridge with Ford Station in the back ground. Of particular note are the substantial embankments on either side of the structure. Note also the houses to the right of the viaduct on the valley floor opposite the park in College Road *6 August 1965*

From the Pasley Street Bridge the very sad sight of the demolition of the viaduct; carried out from the south end so that the spoil could be removed through access to the former Ford Station site. I believe that the contractor who undertook the work thought he was dealing with a masonry structure, and was unprepared for discovering that the arches were actually of cast concrete. I offer no sympathy for carrying out such wanton destruction It is a pity the viaduct could not have been saved. What a wonderful foot and cycle path from Devonport through the two tunnels and then over the St Leaven Valley and along the track bed to Camel's Head it would have all made *20 August 1986*

The present-day view is from Fairfax Terrace, just to the right of the Pasley Street overbridge from which the view is now obscured by growth. The course of the former viaduct can be traced with a good eye as the more modern housing follows the arc of the former railway route. Part of the southern end embankment survives to the left but is heavily overgrown, the only clue that a railway once crossed the valley here. The houses in College Road, mentioned in the top picture, are an excellent link for all three images. *19 April 2015*

A brisk walk over the Pasley Street overbridge and down in to Camperdown Street for this gem of a picture from Sid Sponheimer. In the evening sunshine, and the last week of steam haulage of the train, 34002 'Salisbury' heads off Ford Viaduct with 1V71 1130 Brighton-Plymouth. Particularly noteworthy is the indentation visible on this side of the substantial embankment marking the site of a direct hit by enemy bombing on the first night of the Plymouth Blitz on 21-22 March 1941. Fortunately the railway was soon back in action, but it must be remembered that the whole area being in close proximity to the Dockyard and Naval Base was a target for the Luftwaffe, and much bomb damage was sustained locally. Surprisingly there was little major damage to the railways in the immediate area. *28 August 1964*

What the Luftwaffe failed to do was some 45 years later accomplished by the City Council with demolition of the viaduct and most of the embankment. Due to a combination of fencing and excessive growth, the original viewpoint is impossible to replicate, so the update is just a few feet to the left standing in Camperdown Street. The line of modern housing follows the curve of the viaduct towards what was Ford Station; it is the background streets and houses which provide the best link between the two images. *10 January 2016*

THE BLOCKHOUSE

Welcome to the Blockhouse, one of Plymouth's best-kept secrets. This, the highest point in this area of the City at 227 feet above sea level, offers superb views in all directions. To the south is Plymouth Sound and on a clear day the Eddystone Light, surpassing the view from Plymouth Hoe. To the east is a panorama towards the South Hams, to the north is Dartmoor and its Tors and looking west the hills of South East Cornwall, the Tamar Estuary at its confluence with the River Lynher, and the Dockyard and Naval Base. This is a place with military history and the Mount Pleasant Redoubt of the Napoleonic era marks the summit of this superb public park, in the Second War it was a natural location for anti-aircraft guns.

The Blockhouse also provided a grand stand view of the two railway viaducts over the St Levan Valley, Ford Viaduct being the one nearest the camera, Keyham Viaduct on the Plymouth-Penzance main line is literally just down the road. At the confluence of the Rivers Tamar and Lynher, Royal Navy Ships, probably part of the reserve fleet, lay at anchor. *8 March 1968*

The overall view almost half a century later is pretty much the same but there are some differences, the main one being the removal of the SR Ford Viaduct and the embankments on either side in 1986. Keyham Viaduct is of course still in use, we see 43056 leading 43079 on the rear with 1A81 0844 Penzance-London Paddington. There are changes to some buildings in the Dockyard to accommodate the modern fleet, the latter being a good deal smaller than it was in 1968, reflected by the fact that nothing now lays at anchor where the Rivers Tamar and Lynher meet. *20 April 2015*

The view from St Levan Road looking east, with a nice selection of period cars on show and Keyham Viaduct behind us. On the structure we see a specialised vehicle undertaking an inspection of the viaduct for the City Council, who were at this time considering its future. I could not resist going for the broadside angle as I reckon this was the first movement over Ford Viaduct since the last train had passed over some 20 years earlier. *March 1984*

We move down a few yards towards College Road and in time by a couple of years to see the viaduct at the start of its demolition, a sad sight indeed for such a splendid structure. Particularly eye-catching on the advertising bill boards is the large blue poster with the arrow directing one towards the new Tesco Store at Roborough. The advice is, 'Straight Ahead, 3rd Exit at Roundabout, follow the signs to Tavistock A386', and there is no mention of the five miles in between! *4 August 1986*

The viaduct has vanished, the cars have changed, there are not advertising boards directing one to Tesco or anywhere else and bus passengers no longer have to endure the elements as a modern shelter is provided. Just beyond and opposite the latter, the modern row of houses occupies the space where once the viaduct stood. We shall take a walk to here and turn right up the hill to return to Pasley Street for our exit from the St Levan Valley. *19 April 2015*

At the time of my visit here only one line of rail remained as demolition of the route was well underway, but this is enough to give a good impression of how the rail route, having crossed Ford Viaduct, passed beneath the substantial Pasley Street overbridge to enter the 363 yard Ford Tunnel. It is the south end of this tunnel which passes beneath the already mentioned GWR Devonport Tunnel, the crown of Ford Tunnel being only four feet below the base of the GWR tunnel. The mile between Ford Devon and Devonport Kings Road Stations was one of the most heavily engineered pieces of railway route in the country. *6 August 1965*

Due to access and growth problems, an updated view from the track bed is now impossible, so I have moved on to the Pasley Street overbridge, where the view of the former railway and its tunnel is best described as an untamed jungle. One would not immediately realise the entrance to the tunnel is still there, access to it is now so difficult. Fortunately all the visible houses remain much as they did back in 1965 save for their external décor; the house painters have found much employment here! One wonders with some loving tender care and proper lighting, would not the twin tunnels be an attractive walk/cycle path under Devonport with the unique experience of being able to pass beneath another railway tunnel? *19 April 2015*

Albert Road Halt was situated in the short cutting between Ford and Devonport Park Tunnels and access was by means of a steep path either side of the cutting to reach the required platform. The Halt opened on 1 October 1906, a month before the introduction of the short-lived rail motor service between Friary and St Budeaux. Evidence points to the short station (the platforms were 120 feet in length) being originally of wooden construction, replaced at an unknown date by standard Exmouth Junction (Exeter) concrete materials. The only provision for shelter from the elements for prospective passengers was a GWR type 'Pagoda' on the Plymouth-bound platform. The halt outlived the rail motor services by a good few years closing on 13 January 1947.

By the time of my visit in 1965 lifting of the track was well under way and only one line of rail, the former 'Down' line, was still in situ quietly rusting away, but this is enough to give the impression of the double track main line between the two tunnels. All traces of the halt had vanished many years previously. The view is looking south from the top of Ford Tunnel towards the 534 yard long Devonport Park Tunnel by Kimber's Garage, now Sandwell's Car Centre, mentioned and illustrated on the pages describing Devonport Tunnel on the GWR main line. *6 August 1965*

Imagine my complete surprise in walking up Albert Road to find a suitable gap just to the right of the former Kimber's Garage to update the scene, and not that far out from the original. The cutting is heavily overgrown but the house on the top of Devonport Park Tunnel makes the necessary connection between the two images. The houses to the left are in Exmouth Road, the site of the advertising hoardings seen in the background of the Devonport Albert Road Station pictures, for Albert Road Halt was indeed very close to Devonport Albert Road GWR station. *19 April 2015*

DEVONPORT KINGS ROAD

One emerged from Devonport Park Tunnel to pass beneath the Paradise Road overbridge, the curve marking the limit of the Plymouth, Devonport & South Western Railway, as one reached pure LSWR metals to enter their Devonport Station. Opened on 18 May 1876, trains then entered it from the east as it was the terminus of the short branch from Devonport Junction on the Cornwall Railway, reached from Lydford by running powers over the broad gauge lines. The independent route from Lydford opened on 12 May 1890 for goods and 2 June 1890 for passengers and entered the station from the west direction, the station undergoing major changes with conversion from a terminus to a 'through' station. Trains then went on to terminate at North Road and, from 1 July 1891 until 15 September 1958, at Friary. For a short while the station was known as Devonport & Stonehouse. The suffix 'Kings Road' was added on 26 September 1949. Passenger services were withdrawn with the closure of the SR route from Devonport to St Budeaux, the station reverting to its previous role as a terminus but for goods only for the short branch from Devonport Junction, singled on 26 February 1967, and closed completely on 7 March 1971.

The view looking east from Kings Road after closure to passengers, the scene untidied by dumped track panels but the overall impression is of a grand station. Notice to the right the impressive parcels depot, used as the main parcel base for Plymouth 1956-62 during the rebuilding of North Road Station. *6 August 1965*

The station was demolished in 1971 and the College of Further Education now occupies the site. The updated view was taken a few yards back from the original due to the present day growth by the wall I stood upon back in 1965. *22 March 2015*

In my opinion, Devonport Kings Road was the most elegant and impressive of all the stations in Plymouth. This was a place built to impress and locals felt their station was a real fillip to the pride of the then independent Borough of Devonport. It was designed by WR Galbraith, the LSWR resident engineer, and consisted of two impressive buildings. On the south side was the huge goods shed, while adjoining on the north side was the passenger station which had a twin-ridged glazed roof, whose ironwork (which covered four lines of rail) had come from Belgium at a reported cost of £20,000. This was not a station built on the cheap. Sadly the train shed roofs and end arches suffered badly in the Plymouth Blitz in March and April 1941 and were subsequently replaced by standard SR canopies along with a covered footbridge. The refreshment room situated on the St Budeaux-bound platform survived until September 1962. I recall its daily supply of doughnuts came out from North Road on the 1002 'Atlantic Coast Express'. What a way to send perishables around the City!

The station fronted onto Paradise Road and was accessed by a long, gentle ramp in either direction. Although the station had seen its last passengers the previous year, the exterior view still gave visions of grandeur. The station was constructed with local limestone dressed with Portland stone. Note also, as at Swilly Bridge, the advertising hoardings extol the glories of Guinness. *October 1965*

The present day view from Paradise Road can hardly be described as one containing any impressive buildings. The station was demolished in 1971 and City College now occupies the site. The long approach ramps survive with some original railings. I do feel Devonport lost part of its soul when Kings Road Station was expunged from the scene. *22 March 2015*

DEVONPORT KINGS ROAD

The clock on the Devonport Technical College building behind the station shows it is 1510, so rebuilt West Country Class Pacific 34108 "Wincanton" has arrived on time with the Plymouth portion, and a parcels van attached at Exeter Central, of the 0900 from London Waterloo – with the Plymouth portion and a parcels van attached at Exeter Central – has arrived on time. Of particular interest to the right of the locomotive, the sturdy stone building which bears the legend 'Devonport Mineral Water Company' is the original two road engine shed installed with the opening of the station in May 1876. Its accommodation for locomotives was actually rather limited, which is surprising when one considers how lavish the station was when first built. It not did immediately close when Friary Shed opened in 1898; a couple of engines remained based there for local duties until 1919 when the sidings were removed and the premises were let out commercially. I always feel this picture has captured the aura of the station, the replacement canopies and its robust buildings being shown to good effect. *August 1964*

Almost from the same view point, here's the somewhat depressing scene just seven years after the top picture had been taken. The track has been removed and this fine station awaits the arrival of the demolition crew. To the right in front of the former engine shed stands the impressive water tower, retained when the shed was closed in 1919. Despite the decay and dereliction, the station still stood proud and even at this late stage of its existence, one can still appreciate its size, its buildings and its unique charm. The present day scene will be covered by the 'now' picture on the following page. *March 1971*

We move on to the Paradise Road overbridge at the eastern (Plymouth end) of the station for a general view look west, railway-wise in the direction of St Budeaux.

I suspect many a resident of Devonport and nearby Stonehouse will recall this once familiar scene from this well used thoroughfare, the overall view of Devonport Kings Road station. To the left is the substantial goods shed with its three sloping roofs, beneath which passed the Stonehouse Pool Branch – more of that later. Moving to the right we see the parcels depot behind the station, the latter provided with two through lines and two sidings, the covered footbridge, the substantial station buildings facing Paradise Road and the former engine shed. From this angle, one can appreciate just how large an installation Devonport Kings Road was. The small pile of rubble in the foreground marks the site of the former 37-lever frame signal box, closed on 14 March 1965. From 26 November 1960 this had been a fringe box to the Plymouth Panel, receiving, for the first time in its life, an illuminated diagram. *8 March 1968*

From the precise spot one now has a general view of City College; the station has vanished without trace. Need I say more? Look to the far right of both the pictures and the old Devonport Technical College with its clock tower is the common link. One of the most dramatic changes of scene, I think, on the western side of the City railways. *20 April 2015*

STONEHOUSE POOL JUNCTION

We can join Ivor Hocking in Devonport Kings Road goods yard with the Paradise Road overbridge behind for this portrait of Class 02 30225. The Class had long been synonymous with the former SR lines in the City. I only have records of shed allocations from the summer of 1950 – 30225 was based at Friary from April 1954 until March 1962. 30182, 30183, 30192, 30193 and 30216 will be other numbers no doubt fondly recalled by many. The Class was introduced by Adams in 1889 and 30225 has a construction date of 30 November 1892, making this and 30193 the oldest working engines in daily service in the City at the time. Duties for the Friary-based 02s were mainly Turnchapel Branch (until 1951), Bere Alston-Callington branch, until ousted by the Ivatt tanks in the 1950s, empty stock at Friary and latterly Laira, and the Devonport Kings Road shunt engine which also worked the Stonehouse Pool branch. 30225 was transferred to Eastleigh in March 1962 and withdrawn from service there in December of that year, being cut up in May 1963. Twenty three of the Class were 'exported' to the Isle of Wight by the Southern Railway after the Grouping of 1923, the major changes being the addition of the Westinghouse air brake and its noisy pump and enlarged coal bunkers. It is one of these which has survived in to preservation, W24 'Calbourne'. *September 1961*

Proceeding a few yards under the Paradise Road Bridge, we emerge on the east facing side a decade later than when 30225 was seen quietly simmering away, to witness what to me is a totally depressing scene as track lifting of the Devonport Kings Road site is almost complete. Fortunately the contractors had yet to commence their destruction of the Stonehouse Pool Branch. One can gain a fair impression of what was, not that long before, the physical junction of the line and the start of its descent, at 1-in-40, to pass beneath Devonport Kings Road Goods Yard, as we shall turn around and witness on the following page. The footbridge remains in place over what is now a carpark, and the present day view here will be covered when we come to look at the last passenger train to leave Kings Road. *March 1971*

Railway history is rarely simple, and such is the case with the mile-long Stonehouse Pool Branch. Even this obscure line came in two parts, built by separate companies, and took a decade to complete. The section from Stonehouse Pool Junction to Richmond Walk was opened by the LSWR in 1877, much to the annoyance of the Stonehouse Pool Improvement Company who obtained an Act of Parliament on 13 July 1876 allowing them to construct a quay at Poor Man's Point, and a railway to connect with the LSWR at Richmond Walk. Sir John Aubyn provided the land and urged the LSWR to make the connection. The haggling continued and, coupled with a lack of capital, the 29-chain extension formally opened on 1 March 1886. The LSWR took a perpetual lease on the whole line in August of that year. The line only saw passenger use between April 1904 and May 1910 for Ocean liner traffic whose story I will revisit. The last train, as far as I know, ran in 1966 and the line has a formal closure date of 30 May 1970. Immediately prior to its demolition I undertook a photographic survey of the line which forms the bulk of these pages.

Above is the view peering out of the tunnel at its eastern end looking towards the bridge over Rectory Road.

The line descended steeply from its junction at 1-in-40 and immediately passed under the LSWR Devonport goods yard by a 101 yard tunnel. The picture, right, does portray the imposing grandeur of the LSWR station goods shed.

As will be seen by the other updated views of the line, both these view points are totally inaccessible today. *Both pictures, March 1971*

THE GOODS YARD TUNNEL WEST END

The west end of the 101-yard tunnel under Devonport Kings Road Goods Yard. The tunnel was not straight, being on a 7-chain radius curve, this being readily apparent along with a further illustration of what a fine building and how large the Devonport Kings Road Goods Shed truly was. The line emerged from the tunnel to cross the Rectory Road overbridge whose parapets we see in the foreground. *March 1971*

The scene has changed much over the intervening years with the Devonport Kings Road Goods Shed and the tunnel entrance eradicated by City College. The parapets of the Rectory Road overbridge and the shed on the extreme right confirm this is the precise location for the updated view. This is where the former Stonehouse Pool Branch now becomes a popular footpath for its course down to the half mile or so to the start of Richmond Walk. For our next two comparisons, we will move to the upper left of each picture in to the goods yard for the view looking towards Stonehouse Pool. *22 March 2015*

The view from Devonport Kings Road Goods Yard of the Stonehouse Pool Branch crossing the Rectory Road overbridge, the thoroughfare then taking a right hand turn to run more or less parallel with the railway. The Stonehouse Pool Branch descended here at 1-in-44 on a 9-chain radius curve, perfectly illustrated above. Kings Road is to the right with the pleasure park and its symmetrical footpaths behind, which in my childhood days I recall was the site of a small estate of prefabs. *March 1971*

Re-visiting the site of the former Devonport Kings Road Goods Yard, I was able to find one small gap in the combination of fencing and vegetation to obtain an almost perfect spot for the updated view. The scene is instantly recognisable as the Rectory Road Bridge remains with its modern-day height restriction boards and some greenery, and is one of the few tangible reminders of the railway in the immediate area. The course of the former branch line is clearly discernible. To the left the view towards Stonehouse is relatively clear, giving one a chance to study how that side of the back ground has changed. To the right the bare trees of the top picture beside Kings Road have grown to completely block the view of the park and the houses beyond. *22 March 2015*

PASSING THE BRICKFIELDS

We move on a few yards to where the branch came to run alongside Kings Road. Further to the left, the Technical College Clock Tower just rises above the trees which hide the view of the Brickfields, then as now, a centre for local Athletics. Back in the 1960s it was the venue for many a school sports day. I recall one year my school, St Boniface College, held their annual event there, I think it was 1961. I was sat at the top on the end of a small uncovered grandstand, furnished with my mother's binoculars looking in the opposite direction of the sporting activities as here was a splendid place to view the comings and goings, and the shunting with 30 225, at Devonport Kings Road. While the presentations and speeches were taking place, I was following the 02 on its afternoon sojourn to Stonehouse Pool which came to the attention of more than one of the school masters. I was told to report the Head Master (Brother Grice) the next day, who was not impressed "by my plainly visible non interest and public disregard of school activities", and ordered to one hour of detention. A price I though well worth paying for such an afternoon of entertainment. The only other time I received detention was for riding my bicycle over a prefect's foot! *March 1971*

The curve of the former line, Kings Road to the left and the houses to the right, provide a common link to a picture where the background has been transformed by the College of Further Education replacing the station goods yard. As for The Brickfields, these prosper as a major centre for athletics and since 2003 have also been the home of Plymouth Albion Rugby Union Football Club. There is no danger now of spectators being distracted by passing trains and school sports days can pass off unhindered. *22 March 2015*

We turn around and look in the opposite direction to find the railway line following the contours of the creek, curving away towards Richmond Walk on a perfect 'S' bend. Kings Road and the park are to the right, it is the left hand background which provides the most interest; we catch a glimpse of Stonehouse Bridge built by John Smeaton of Eddystone Lighthouse fame and completed in 1773. It was a toll bridge until 1924, the cost for a pedestrian to pass over was a halfpenny, and to this day despite the structure being hidden on its north side by reclamation, it is still known locally as Ha'penny Bridge. Behind this on the other side of the creek we see some well remembered Stonehouse buildings; the old Regent Brewery with its tower stands out, to its left the remains of the Stonehouse/Devonport Power Station, and towering above is the Grain Silo in Millbay Docks. *10 July 1967*

The 'S' bend of the former railway line, with a glimpse of the park through the now well-grown saplings of the 1960s on the right by Kings Road, provide an unmistakable link between the two images. The washing line and any view of the now filled in creek are blocked by growth, which also obscures a much changed view. The Regent Brewery and the power station areas have all been redeveloped as we glimpse the buildings of today and the Millbay Grain Silo, demolished in 2008, no longer towers above. A careful eye will just pick out the green embankment now blocking Stonehouse Bridge. This section of the former railway survives as a pleasant footpath. *22 March 2015*

THE VIEW FROM THE A374

A gem of a view from my old friend Keith Holt, taken off the A374 bridge which depicts the Stonehouse Pool Branch running alongside the yet to be in filled Stonehouse Creek. At this time the waters still reached Millbridge and, as we have seen until the 1890s, they reached Pennycomequick, giving us this wonderful panorama. To the left is the rear of the grandstand of the rectory, the home of Devonport Services Rugby Union Club, moving to the right the building with the long colonnade is the old military hospital building, built in 1797. In 1963 this was split between Tamar Central School and Devonport High School for Boys. In 1990 Tamar, which had become co-educational in 1972, was closed, and the whole site was taken over by Devonport High School for Boys. The hospital had been earmarked for use as an educational establishment in1939 but the outbreak of World War II halted that process temporarily. *April 1963*

My variation of the view a couple of years later is taken slightly further to the left. There are a number of features which stand out; railway-wise one can fully appreciate the 'S'bend which took the Stonehouse Pool Branch from Rectory Road to Richmond Walk. To the top left, although mostly hidden by a tree, one can pick out the Devonport Kings Road Goods Shed. Look to the right of the latter towards the Rectory Rugby Ground Grandstand, and the top of the arches of the Paradise Road Bridge just to the east of Kings Road Station can be picked out. This is where we saw 30225 resting between duties. *October 1965*

The view moves on by six years and times are changing. Despite a new bridge built to span it, the railway line was by now officially closed and awaiting demolition. The presence of the rails was not an obstacle in provision of access to aid a scheme that would change the whole area for ever: the infilling of Stonehouse Creek. As can be seen, this was now underway and would be completed the following year. Soon no longer would a railway pass this way, nor would the waters reach Millbridge again. On Kings Road we still get an uninterrupted view looking up towards Kings Road Station and the Paradise Road Bridge. *March 1971*

Another location where it is very hard to believe this is the same place. The railway has been eradicated, and on the reclaimed land, where once the railway curved beside the waters, now stands the Stonehouse Creek Leisure & Social Club, a misnomer in some ways as there is little evidence the creek ever existed on this side of the dual carriageway. This social club blocks the view of the Rectory Rugby Ground, which is still in use, and much of the still-extant housing. Tree growth blocks any decent view of the panorama enjoyed here half a century ago. *20 April 2015*

JUST BY STONEHOUSE BRIDGE

Between the western end of Stonehouse Bridge and the start of Devonport Hill, the Stonehouse Pool Branch passed beneath the A374 road. The highway here, until October 1961, was the A38 following its course to the Torpoint Ferry. It was rerouted via Saltash on the opening of the Tamar Road Bridge. This section of the A374 was upgraded to a dual carriageway in the late 1960s, in the process greatly altering the appearance of Stonehouse Bridge. Although the Stonehouse Pool Branch was at the time moribund – the last train had run over it in June 1966 – in 1967 plans were announced to construct an oil terminal at Stonehouse Quay, thus giving the line a long term future. Accordingly the new dual carriageway was built with a new concrete bridge alongside the still existing masonry structure at the Richmond Walk/Kings Road/Devonport Hill Junction to accommodate the railway line. However, the Middle East went to war and the Stonehouse Pool Branch was an unfortunate casualty. As far as I know, a train never did pass beneath the newly extended structure.

The new concrete bridge over the line; the rusty rails of the railway it was built to cross await the demolition crew. *March 1971*

That smart new concrete bridge has now weathered somewhat, the footpath follows the course of the former railway with some minor alterations to the levels and trees have grown but for once do not spoil the view. Add in a new lamppost on the former railway and a modern day directions board for the road and, yes, the changes are many but at this angle the scene here is still recognisable, which, as we saw on the two previous pages, was not the case when we observed the view from the A374. *20 April 2015*

Local history and railway history have two things in common – neither is simple or straight-forward. Take for example the busiest station in Europe: Clapham Junction but a mile from Clapham yet it is actually sited in the district of Battersea. The Stonehouse Pool Branch was a quiet outpost of the SR, which like Clapham Junction never actually penetrated its namesake borough. Here the boundary between Devonport and East Stonehouse ran up the centre of the creek to Millbridge so the whole of the line was entirely in Devonport. Another thought: 180 trains an hour can be seen at peak times passing through Clapham Junction; it would have taken about three months to see the same number of trains passing under the once A38 road now the A374 where it meets Kings Road and Richmond Walk!

It is a simple stroll under the A374 to reach the south side of the bridge which looks very different to its northern portal as we see the original masonry arch built to pass beneath the road at the start of Devonport Hill. As we have seen the 1960's extension on the north side was of concrete construction. Richmond Walk is to the top right. *March 1971*

The south side of the bridge today marks the end of the footpath on the former railway from Rectory Road. Beyond here the track bed is lost under redevelopment. It is the bridge itself which survives as the main link between the two images; everything has changed beyond recognition. All traces of the railway have vanished with its former route blocked by a wall with a very high fence. At a slightly higher level, the footpath veers away from the course of the former branch line to join Richmond Walk. *20 April 2015*

THE RAILWAY AT RICHMOND WALK, LOOKING SOUTH

The view is from Richmond Walk looking just from the south of the A374 bridge towards the terminus at Stonehouse Pool. The railway here took a brief course on a more gradual 'S' bend behind the industrial buildings on Richmond Walk, towards the rather fine masonry bridge we see in the near distance. This, a pedestrian only bridge, will be our next port of call. Just beyond the bridge were Jewson's Timber Saw Mills and I recall that Scaffold Great Britain also had a base on Richmond Walk around this time. The area had a much more industrial look about it in those bygone days. *March 1971*

The view from the same spot much changed from that above, there is no evidence that a railway line once passed through here. To the right much greenery has appeared on the cliff face, the track bed has been overtaken by a somewhat untidy industrial estate and trees obscure any view to the right. Although now not visible from this angle, the masonry footbridge from Richmond Walk to Mount Wise survives, so time to amble down Richmond Walk and stand upon it for a further aspect of the changes in the area. *20 April 2015*

We have moved down the few yards to the pedestrian bridge for the view looking north towards the A374 Road Bridge with Richmond Walk, where the two pictures on the previous page were taken from, visible beyond the works premises to the right. The principal feature of the picture is the large stone outcrop to the left, on whose summit in 1779 the Bluff Battery redoubt was established as part of the outer defences for the Naval Dockyard. *March 1971*

If one is into Cherry Pickers, this is the place for you as the course of the former railway has been replaced by the yard of LTC Fork Rental. Whilst the view of the railway and Richmond Walk has been transformed, the large stone outcrop survives with added greenery. Bluff Battery is a Devon County Geological Site whose top is accessible from Devonport Hill. The quarried outcrops have much to interest the geologist, a subject beyond the scope of this book. *20 April 2015*

THE RAILWAY AT RICHMOND WALK

The view from the pedestrian overbridge looking the other way from Bluff Battery as the railway proceeded alongside Jewson's Timber Saw Mills to the left and under Mount Wise Park on the right towards the loop line just around the corner, which we shall reach on the next page. Notice the wooden plank placed on the rails. This was an indication that demolition work was in progress a little further ahead, so I only really made it just in time to make this detailed record of the Stonehouse Pool Branch. The updated view of this location is presented on the following page. *March 1971*

We shall see that the only intermediate loop on the line started immediately around the corner from here, where one found this sign informing railway staff that 'N' and 'N1' Class engines must not pass this point on either loop line. We saw an 'N' at Ford on the 0730 Yeoford Goods; the 'N1' was a slightly more powerful version. Some background information on the working of the line may be relevant at this point, and I quote some extracts from the Southern Railway Western Appendices to the Working Time Tables dated 26 March 1934. "*This line, which is worked as a siding, connects with Devonport goods yard by means of hand points which lie normally kept for the goods yard. 'N' and 'N1' Class engines may be permitted to work over the Stonehouse Pool Line as between Devonport Station and a point 100 yards on the wharf side of Richmond Walk Level Crossing, at which notice boards are fixed*". Use of any engine larger than an '02' was unknown certainly in the post war era, but the sign stood proud to the end. I tried to purchase the sign from the contractors but, when I was able to find the right man to speak to, it had already been put on the bonfire. What a reminder of the line this would have been. *March 1971*

A further view from behind Richmond Walk looking towards the A374 Bridge, taken standing on the railway bank, showing the south side of the pedestrian bridge and a much more impressive view of Bluff Battery. Jewson's Timber Saw Mills are to the right. *March 1971*

It is impossible to update this precise angle today due to the site being occupied by the timber merchant, growth and fencing, so instead of the updated view looking back towards the bridge, this is the view from the bridge looking back to the original view point which was on the bank behind the end of the large PSE timber shed on the right. This picture also fulfils the role of updating the view from the bridge looking towards Stonehouse Pool on the previous page. The whole scene has changed out of recognition with the railway and the industries it served are just a memory. All that remains is the pedestrian footbridge and it is not the easiest place from which to obtain an updated view as although access is not a problem, both sides are covered high above each parapet with what is best described as an ugly iron cage resembling the bars of a prison cell. This was the only suitable gap I could find on this side of it to take a picture, it must be said the one on the other side looking at the cherry picker yard was of equal challenge. *20 April 2015*

RICHMOND WALK LOOP

Immediately around the corner from passing beneath the pedestrian footpath lay the only intermediate siding on the line, known officially as James Bros Sidings, the latter being timber merchants. Although built in the style of a loop, this was not a passing place as only one train at a time was permitted on the line: this was a siding which could be accessed from either end. History does not give a precise date for its opening, but it was recorded by the Devonport SR Station Master in November 1927 that a new loop had been constructed adjacent to an admiralty store on the north side of Richmond Walk Level Crossing.

The view of the loop looking towards Stonehouse Pool as demolition of the line gets under way with the point work here already disturbed. This is where the sad task begun. Despite the poor light and some growth not helping, one can gain a good enough impression of the scene at this end of the loop. For the updated view of this location see the top picture on the previous page. *March 1971*

Taken from Richmond Walk Level Crossing, this is the view looking towards Kings Road as the contractors are starting work on removal of the south end points, but at least enough still survived for me to record the simple track layout out. Note in the background straddling the line is the loading gauge, the principal of which was explained when one was encountered on the Bull Point Branch. *March 1971*

The only piece of straight track on the Stonehouse Pool Branch was the short section which crossed Richmond Walk on the level, the level crossing gates being worked by the train crew, although there was a signal box here until 1 February 1928. The view is looking towards Kings Road, the south end of James Bros Siding, is immediately beyond the level crossing. The gates I always thought were rather ornate. The Southern Railway 1934 Western Appendices state: "*The gates at Richmond Walk Level Crossing are maintained normally across the railway, secured in this position by hand bolts and padlocks, and trains proceeding from Devonport to Stonehouse Pool must be brought to a stand well clear of the level crossing and the brakes applied.*" On the return journey, once the train had passed back over the crossing and gates had been replaced across the railway, the man in charge would, by use of the telephone provided here, contact the Devonport Signalman for permission to proceed. With hindsight I should have removed the contractor's trailer, but fortunately it does not really interfere with the view. *March 1971*

The sole remaining piece of track of the former Stonehouse Pool Branch is a couple of rails in the road where the railway used to cross Richmond Walk on the level. The view is again looking towards Kings Road, with the background hill a useful reference point to link the two images. The stone wall blocks any view (and access to) the former James Bros Siding. Behind the photographer is the entrance to the Stonehouse Pool Terminus, the line beyond this point incidentally had been transferred to the British Transport Docks Board as from 31 December 1960. *20 April 2015*

STONEHOUSE POOL

We reach the water's edge at Stonehouse Pool where the quay provided an average of 22-24 feet of water (18 feet at spring low tides) and ships of up to 2,000 tons could berth. Cargoes were discharged direct into railway wagons placed alongside, but the traffic was never heavy. When the extension to Stonehouse Pool was completed, a small station was erected on the quay. There was not at any time a local passenger service on the line, but it did come into its own for a short period in the Edwardian era when fierce competition raged between the GWR and the LSWR for the lucrative ocean traffic from Plymouth. This took off in 1904 when the LSWR made good use of its ready made alternative to Millbay and, on 9 April of that year, the Ocean Terminal was opened here. Similar to Admiralty Platform and Millbay Ocean Terminal, it did not appear in public timetables. Passengers – the mails were left to the GWR – from ships anchored in Plymouth Sound, were taken to Stonehouse Pool and whisked off to London in the finest stock of the day. In 1908 the stock was augmented by the only sleeping cars the LSWR ever possessed, but this intense period of rivalry would be short lived as economics overtook prestige and the Ocean Traffic ended here in May 1910, the Stonehouse Pool Branch reverting to its more normal role as a quiet goods-only railway byway. The GWR bought the sleeping cars.

The remains of the passenger platform and some overgrown track present a sad scene of dereliction and decay in this view looking towards Devonport Kings Road. *22 October 1965*

Such are the changes here all traces of the railway and its Ocean Terminal have been completely expunged, this is now a view from the Mayflower Marina looking towards the Princess Yachts' base. Look just to the right of the latter for the spire of St Peter's Church in Wyndham Street. This with the houses to the extreme right confirm the location. *20 April 2015*

The view looking towards the stop blocks at Stonehouse Pool, the former and rather forlorn passenger platform still readily apparent. It was hard to imagine even when I stood here in 1965 that that this was once an Ocean Terminal, built on a 350-foot-long curved island platform with buildings which contained facilities for customs, baggage, booking and telegraph offices, waiting rooms, toilets and refreshment bar, the latter only offering light snacks as passengers were expected to dine on the boat train. The buildings were subsequently used as stores and a Quay Master's house – sadly they were a casualty of the Plymouth Blitz in March 1941. The site was taken over by the US Navy in 1944 as the quay played its part in the D Day preparations. After the war the quay returned to its role as a quiet freight railway terminus. The two sidings were used by Blight & White Engineering and the Sulfo Phosphate Company, supplemented by inward coal traffic and Jewson's timber. Traffic had mostly ceased by the mid-1960s and the rusty rails indicate little use at this time. *22 October 1965*

The Mayflower Marina opened in 1971 on the site of the railway terminus and its development has greatly altered the topography of the whole area. All traces of the original quay and any railway presence are impossible to find. Here I must record my thanks to the very helpful staff of the marina who went out of their way to provide guidance and access to the best spots to update the pictures. It was their suggestion to use the small fortification at Cremyll on the other side of the River Tamar (look just above the railings by the leaning pole in the top picture and between the masts on the extreme left of the lower picture) and the Cornish hills beyond to provide any link between the two images. *20 April 2015*

Following its brief role as a passenger-carrying line in the Edwardian era, during the battle between the GWR and LSWR for the ocean traffic, the quay reverted to its former role as a goods only depot in 1910. Subsequently passenger trains were few and far between. Some naval specials are known to have run but precise dates and times, as far as I know, went unrecorded and are now lost in the mists of time.

Certainly in the post war era, the only two known passenger-carrying trains to run down to Stonehouse Pool were two Rail Tours both run by the Plymouth Railway Circle, and both were Goods Brake Van specials. The first was on 14 May 1960 with Class 02 30193. A black and white illustration of this appears in my book 'Steaming Around Plymouth', published by History Press. The second was the Plymouth area Brake Van Tour of June 1966, hauled by Class 03 D2177. Whilst this was not quite the luxury of the ocean saloons of the Edwardian era, it was a most enjoyable way to travel.

Due to the failure of D2178 in Millbay Docks (as we have seen), the train was very late by the time it reached Stonehouse Pool in fading light, not helped by the sun too far round, pushing 50 ASA Agfa colour film to its limits. It is high tide as passengers inspect the former Ocean Terminal. This was certainly the last passenger train to traverse the line, and may well have been the last of all as the final revenue-earning train is recorded as running in the same month.

Poor Man's Point became the Stonehouse Pool Terminus of a little railway immortalised for its part in the Ocean Liner battle. Looking at all the fashionable craft on show in the Mayflower Marina, Poor Man's Point has come a long way; it would certainly not be an apt description in this day and age. The line was a mile long and what a story it has to tell. So now it is back to Devonport Kings Road to cast eyes over the last passenger train to grace its platforms, and this remarkably will take us back to the era of Edwardian saloons. *18 June 1966*

After closure to passengers in September 1964, a couple of Rail Tours ran out from Devonport Junction but only to or via the yard. To the best of my knowledge, only one further passenger train entered the former platforms and it was a Royal one, conveying the Duke of Edinburgh. The train was worked down from London through the night by D1023 'Western Fusilier' to Devonport Kings Road where it was securely stabled. D821 'Greyhound' was then attached to the rear to later return the train to Plymouth so HRH could arrive at a civilised hour. Thus at 1010 the Royal Party departed behind D821, and in the process became the last passengers to leave the station. A right Royal farewell one could say, Royal 'last trains' are few and far between and, surprisingly, I was the lone photographer here to record the event. *8 March 1968*

While on the subject of the last rites at Devonport Kings Road as seen from Paradise Road, this is the rather forlorn station information board here on the last day of passenger services. Still proclaiming its Southern heritage, potential passengers are offered direct trains to Exeter, Portsmouth, Brighton and London. A reminder the LSWR originally built their grand station partly to impress the Admiralty and win the lucrative traffic to and from the south coast. Even the advert below for the fast 'Golden Hind' service on the rival former GWR route from Plymouth to Paddington, introduced just three months before, is starting to peel away. *6 September 1964*

STONEHOUSE POOL JUNCTION

The Royal Train passes the junction with the Stonehouse Pool Branch. The formation is D821 with saloons 5155, 799 built by the LMS in 1941, 9007 built by the GWR in 1945, 5154, and on the rear steam heat van DW12387. 5154 and 5155 were built as special saloons by the London & North Western Railway in 1905, recalling the era of the saloons that passed this way in the battle for the ocean traffic, and converted to Royal use in 1924. These were the last clearstory roof stock to be seen in the City. All four of these splendid vehicles survive in preservation under the auspices of the National Railway Museum. Not authorised for running and certainly not as part of the Royal Train was DW12387. The boiler on D821 had failed and in those days of steam heating, the local manager made the decision that the Royal Party had to be kept comfortable and the steam heating van, normally used to warm the sleeping cars, was added at Plymouth on the outward run. HQ were not impressed; the manager concerned was taken to task, issues raised and questions asked. Suffice to say the Royal Party stayed nice and warm, and the manager concerned continued to manage, and did so for a good decade or more I seem to recall. *8 March 1968*

Where once the Stonehouse Pool Branch met the main line, and the Duke of Edinburgh and the steam heating van made history in 1968, there is now a large carpark to serve City College. The obvious link between the two images is the pedestrian footbridge which connects Providence Place and Wilton Road. Just out of camera range on its right is the Mother Church of Devonport, Stoke Damerel where my parents were married and my sister and I were christened. A very special place for my family and once right beside the railway! To the left, the bank still has a railway appearance and the houses make another link between the two pictures. *20 April 2015*

This is the view from the Fitzroy Road overbridge which lay just to the east of the Stonehouse Pool Junction looking towards Devonport Junction. As the line awaited the cutter's torch, this was a last chance to study what had not long before been a double-track main line. Here it was on a gentle 20-chain left hand curve on a falling gradient towards the station of 1-in-330. This, of course, was part of the branch which opened in 1876 to take the LSWR into its own terminus in Devonport, closed to passengers in September 1964 and was singled from Devonport Junction to Devonport Kings Road on 26 February 1967 although most of the redundant former 'Up' line remained in situ and finally closed on 7 March 1971. The nearest of the two masonry arches is the Valletort Road Bridge, just beyond is the more substantial Molesworth Road Bridge, from which it is just a short hop to the next location, a return to Devonport Junction. *March 1971*

Standing in the same spot today, one would have no indication whatsoever that there was ever a double track railway here. I found my bearings by using part of the parapet of the former railway bridge, and the bend of the road, to establish without doubt that I was standing where I did back in 1971. This really is the same place. *20 April 2015*

DEVONPORT JUNCTION

So we return by former Southern metals to Devonport Junction, completing 'a figure of 8' journey from here out on the GWR to Saltash and back from the banks of the Tamar by the SR. Having entwined their separate ways through the City's western suburbs, here the two railways met for the last lap in to Plymouth North Road. Notice how the GWR line drops down towards the junction at 1-in-59, the Southern line rising gently towards it at 1-in-94. Our views on this and the next page are from the Wingfield Way Bridge, already visited on our outward journey, which lay by the 230 mile post from London Waterloo. The mileage here from Paddington on the direct route via Westbury is 226 miles and 22 chains.

Class 42 'Warship' D808 'Centaur' is displaying the wrong head code approaching Devonport Junction with 1A94 1400 Penzance-London Paddington. This picture was taken the day before the double track to Devonport Kings Road was reduced to one operational track. *25 February 1967*

D 1023 'Western Fusilier' returning light engine from Kings Road having worked the Royal Train for the Duke of Edinburgh over night from London and, like the Royal saloons she brought down that night, she is also preserved by the National Railway Museum. Despite the double-track appearance the SR line was, by this time, worked as a single line to Kings Road over the former 'Down' line, while the former 'Up' line was put out of use. The difference in height and gradient of the two lines as each passes beneath Molesworth Road is quite marked from this angle as we move to the south end of the Wingfield Way Bridge. *8 March 1968*

As time draws on, here are two further views of the scene from the south end of the Wingfield Way overbridge as it evolved at Devonport Junction with regard to the former SR line.

The former Southern line to Devonport Kings Road was lifted in 1971. Here in the following year we see an unidentified Class 25 diesel heading west light engine on the GWR main line towards Devonport Albert Road. The former SR main line was by this time a demolished railway, the empty track bed a poignant reminder of the past, but at least one could still appreciate where it once ran. *26 September 1972*

The former SR route here is no more: it has been infilled to provide a nice piece of green open space. One would never know there was once a railway cutting here, such are the changes coupled with the growth and, but for the road on the extreme left, I cannot really find anything to link this and the previous three pictures of this location. The GWR route, as we have previously noted climbs away up Devonport Bank towards Albert Road, and of course is still there but now hidden at this angle by the excessive growth to the right. At least if one stands in this precise spot today and muses over the lost railway here, one can at least hear a train pass by very close. *4 March 2015*

DEVONPORT JUNCTION

We just turn around on the Wingfield Way Bridge and look the other way towards Cornwall Junction and Plymouth North Road. We have visited this location in our travels out on the GWR route looking at the view from the extreme south end of the bridge. Here we stand mid way along it seeing how the scene has changed over half a century.

An historic view of Devonport Junction on the last day, it was a junction between two double track railways and the line in to Kings Road was singled the following day. D808 'Centaur' and the 1400 Penzance-London Paddington head for Plymouth; captured by my camera in exactly the same place we saw the picture of the three-coach auto train from Saltash in 1960. *25 February 1967*

'Warship meets Western', a gem from the Diesel Hydraulic era to make many a railway enthusiast drool with nostalgia. On the former GWR line Class 43 'Warship' D839 'Relentless' passes by with 1A48 0755 Penzance-London Paddington. It is interesting to note the working timetable of the day shows this train as far as Plymouth booked for D8XX Class with a load of 245 tons. On the now singled former Southern Line Class 52 D1023 'Western Fusilier', running light engine Devonport Kings Road to Laira Depot after working the Royal Train, awaits the signal to proceed. *8 March 1968*

The 'Warship' era was short, it lasted but 14 years, yet this period was to witness great changes on our railway system with the end of steam, rationalisation and line closures, the latter usually followed by demolition and decay. One of numerous locations to undergo such a transition in such a short space of time was Devonport Junction as our third picture of the 'Warship' era here proves.

One of the final duties for the Class was to work the 'Down' 'Cornishman' forward from Plymouth to Penzance. Class 42 'Warship' D806 'Cambrian' makes a fine sight with this train, 1V72 0735 Leeds-Penzance, passing the by now former Devonport Junction. The former Southern route had been lifted the previous year. The main differences between a Class 42 and a Class 43 'Warship' were that the 42s were built by British Rail at Swindon, the 43s by the North British Company in Scotland, and putting it in simple terms, they had different power units. The 'Warship' era would end within three months of this picture being taken. *26 September 1972*

The 'Warship' age is a dim and distant memory here, as is that of when two main lines converged here. Excessive growth has overtaken the course of the former SR route and it is hard to tell that this really was a junction. Ever constant in all four pictures is the background housing, with the flats in Wingfield Road opposite the junction particularly prominent. As these flats undergo some restoration work, 'Sprinter' 150 232 passes by with 2P86 1141 Penzance-Plymouth. *4 March 2015*

There is a saying that every picture tells a story – well this one tells more than most. Taken by Dave Down, a prolific local photographer I knew well, it is a close up view of Cornwall Loop Junction; we saw a more general view from North Road West on our journey out from Millbay heading west. What makes this picture so historic is its date, the penultimate day of services over the former SR route from Devonport Junction to St Budeaux. Dave is riding behind 41317 on the last 2C78 1614 Plymouth-Tavistock North, a train which until 1961 ran to Brentor, and is passing 1A94 1355 Penzance-London Paddington, thought to be hauled by D869, but that is subject to confirmation. Plymouth-Tavistock North locals would become DMUs in the recasting of the timetable taking effect two days later, which also marked the end of regular steam working in Plymouth, although one train originating from Okehampton and the odd freight would last for about another six weeks or so. The colour light signal controlled by the Plymouth Panel Box has the dual role of protecting the former Cornwall Loop Junction and showing the route setting for Devonport Junction. The 'feather' above the green light, with its white strip of lights illuminated, is the indication for the route being set for Devonport Kings Road, and that is what makes this picture so special. There is another interesting feature worthy of mention in the view and that is to the right, beside train 1A94. I refer to the back lane of the houses in Whittington Street which marks the site of the temporary Exhibition Sidings, installed for a short period in 1865 and again in 1872 from Devonport Junction into Central Park, crossing Alma Road on the level, for the Bath & West Show. The mind can only boggle at the paperwork and the consultants involved for any such temporary construction today. *AC/BM Collection, 5 September 1964*

Close-up photography of Cornwall Loop Viaduct on the south side only became possible after the Locomotive Servicing Point was removed, the ground filled in and levels raised to create the park and thus public access here. This was illustrated when we viewed the scene from North Road West on our journey out from Millbay.

The sole 'Provincial' liveried Class 47, 47 475 provides assistance to an ailing (and late running) DMU working the 0750 Penzance-Plymouth, a rare sight as this engine was not often seen in the area. The locomotive only carried this livery for three years, from Spring 1989 until August 1992, after which it was repainted in the Rail Express red livery. Note the piers of the former Stonehouse Pool Viaduct to the left. *March 1991*

'Split box' 37 350, i.e. the head code, would be displayed in two halves in the box either side of the bonnet, repainted in its original green livery with the addition of small yellow warning panels, also bearing its original number D6700, for this was the first Class 37 to be built. It is working 6C43 (not 1N83 as displayed in the split boxes) 1333 St Blazey-Exeter Riverside, the Polybulks on their way to the Potteries. This engine spent about a month on these duties before the Class 66s took over. D6700 is now preserved by the NRM as part of the National Collection. The Polybulks still run albeit only once a week, the only regular freight traffic to pass through Plymouth. After the Dawlish sea wall collapse in February 2014, this flow returned to the rails immediately upon the line reopening. It was stated that at least 49 heavy Lorries were needed to convey this traffic by road. *14 April 1999*

In the intervening two years between this and the picture of D6700, there is an addition to the scene; the steel sculpture by Richard Deacon has been placed on the piers of the former Stonehouse Pool Viaduct. There is also more growth, a sign of things to come. An annual treat is the visit of the 'Orient Express' to the West Country in April of each year, bringing a slice of glamour to the local rails. Pullman Cars would have been seen here for a short while after World War II. The 'Devon Belle' all-Pullman train from Waterloo to Ilfracombe and Plymouth was introduced on 20 June 1947, but the four-coach Plymouth portion lasted only until September 1949 due to lack of demand. Perhaps post war austerity Britain was not the right time for such luxury? Royal train locomotive 47 799 'Prince Harry' has charge of 1Z88 1330 Truro-London Victoria. Behind the locomotive are two luggage coaches ahead of the splendid Pullman Cars which make an impressive sight as the end of the train stretches back to Devonport Junction. *29 April 2001*

Few locomotives, let alone celebrity ones, pass through here at the present time; indeed on some days the only locomotive to pass through here would be the one on the 'Night Riviera' with its sleeping cars on the journey from Penzance to Paddington, such are the changes on the rails. Off the rails, such is the growth of vegetation here coupled with an awkward fence that it is now extremely difficult to obtain a decent picture at this location. After some exploration I did find just one gap in the North Road jungle. Sprinter 150 121 heads west with 2C47 1349 Plymouth-Penzance; one can see enough of the viaduct and some of the background houses to link this and the previous three pictures. I suspect it will not be long before this view is gone forever. *4 March 2015*

The provision of the public open space here also meant that a closer view of the Cornwall Loop looking towards Plymouth Station became possible. The site of the former Locomotive Servicing Point is behind the photographer. On its summer holidays in the West Country, Midland Main Line livery HST with 43076 out of sight on the front and 43077 is seen here on the rear approach to Plymouth Station with the Newquay-Leeds. The MML set was borrowed by Cross Country to supplement provision of stock for the enhanced summer Saturday service. The former Royal Mail Sorting Office in Pennycomequick stands out well to the left of 43077. The Midland Main Line franchise was created upon privatisation on 28 April 1996 and was run by National Express. This was combined with some Central Trains services to form East Midland Trains run by Stagecoach as from 11 November 2007, so yet another livery has passed in to the history book. *29 August 1998*

Such is the growth of the trees at this point in the park that it is very difficult to even see the railway from here that is but a few yards to the left. Fortunately the station tower block rises above the foliage, just, and setting that to the top right of the view does indeed confirm this is the same location. Any former railway use of the site, and in the process any enjoyment of the view towards Central Park or anywhere else, has been completely obliterated. *4 March 2015*

PLYMOUTH STATION HEADING WEST

So our journey ends where it began in the platforms of Plymouth Station. The view is looking east; the two trains are ready to head west. Each will run over a different route out of the City in opposite directions and each is a service that no longer runs.

I had just been for an interview with Mr Savoury, the then Station Master, prior to joining the railway. His office was on Platform 2, I came out to find 34054 'Lord Beaverbrook' standing in Platform 3 with the 1110 to Brighton. I would join the railway within weeks, 34 054 would be withdrawn five months later and in due course the popular through service to the south coast would cease. This is a traffic flow sadly neglected by the privatised railway of today. *20 April 1964*

The milk trains were a staple traffic of the railway but the last would run in August 1979. I had drawn the short straw for the night turn on New Year's Eve and 1977 would be the last year for the Westerns. Only five remained as the New Year dawned and at about 0230 D1048 'Western Lady' ran into Platform 5 with the 0300 'Down' milk empties. Time to celebrate the New Year in a unique way – time exposures of the milk empties! D1048 has passed in to railway preservation and is still with us, unlike many of the trains and scenes recorded in this book. I hope you have enjoyed the journey through past and present. *1 January 1977 at about 0245!*